MORRIS

0 1022 0412649 8

W9-CJJ-046

El Salvador

Richard Arghiris

DISCARDED

The Morristown & Morris Township Library
One Miller Rd.
Morristown, NJ 07960

Credits

Footprint credits

Editor: Felicity Laughton
Production and layout: Emma Bryers
Maps: Kevin Feeney

Managing Director: Andy Riddle
Commercial Director: Patrick Dawson
Publisher: Alan Murphy
Publishing Managers: Felicity Laughton,
Nicola Gibbs
Digital Editors: Jo Williams, Tom Mellors
Marketing and PR: Liz Harper
Sales: Diane McEntee
Advertising: Renu Sibal
Finance and Administration:
Elizabeth Taylor

Photography credits

Front cover: Andre Nantel / Shutterstock
Back cover: Andre Nantel / Shutterstock

Printed in Great Britain by CPI Antony Rowe,
Chippenham, Wiltshire

MIX
Paper from
responsible sources
FSC® C013604
www.fsc.org

Every effort has been made to ensure that
the facts in this guidebook are accurate.
However, travellers should still obtain advice
from consulates, airlines, etc, about travel
and visa requirements before travelling.
The authors and publishers cannot accept
responsibility for any loss, injury or
inconvenience however caused.

Publishing information

Footprint *Focus El Salvador*
1st edition
© Footprint Handbooks Ltd
November 2011

ISBN: 978 1 908206 42 8
CIP DATA: A catalogue record for this book
is available from the British Library

® Footprint Handbooks and the
Footprint mark are a registered
trademark of Footprint Handbooks Ltd

Published by Footprint
6 Riverside Court
Lower Bristol Road
Bath BA2 3DZ, UK
T +44 (0)1225 469141
F +44 (0)1225 469461
footprinttravelguides.com

Distributed in the USA by Globe Pequot Press,
Guilford, Connecticut

All rights reserved. No part of this publication
may be reproduced, stored in a retrieval
system, or transmitted, in any form or by any
means, electronic, mechanical, photocopying,
recording, or otherwise without the prior
permission of Footprint Handbooks Ltd.

The content of Footprint *Focus El Salvador*
has been taken directly from Footprint's
Central America Handbook which was
researched and written by Richard Arghiris
and Peter Hutchison.

Contents

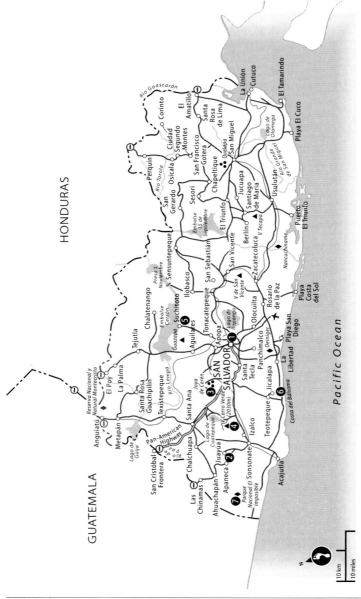

El Salvador is a lively country and the people are just as friendly – some say more so – than in the rest of Central America. Ornately painted and colourful buses bump from place to place, just as they do in Guatemala and Honduras, but El Salvador has better roads and the quality of the buses is superior to that of neighbouring countries. While the rest of Central America relies on tortillas, Salvadoreans fill them with beans, cheese or meat and call them *pupusas*. Pinning it down is difficult but there's a slightly different feel here from neighbouring countries.

Guidebooks tend to urge caution, but in reality El Salvador is no more dangerous than other Central American countries. During the civil war, Salvadoreans sought refuge abroad; now they're returning, bringing with them a gang culture and other less-than-favourable imports from the United States, although as a tourist you are rarely subjected to any of these social problems.

Despite the high rate of gang-related crime, frequent natural disasters and a tourist infrastructure less developed than its neighbouring countries, there are some compelling reasons why you should visit El Salvador: dramatic volcanic landscapes, blue-green lagoons, horizon-filling panoramas and golden beaches. In the northern hills around El Poy and Perquín the trekking is divine, with far-reaching views across staggered horizons. The stark cinder cone of Volcán Izalco offers a challenging but rewarding trek from the slopes of Cerro Verde, while El Imposible National Park provides the chance to visit a forest. Along the coast, choose from surfing, diving or simply lazing around and watching the endless display of Pacific sunsets.

Planning your trip

Life in El Salvador focuses on San Salvador. All roads lead towards the capital with just a few exceptions. Planning your trip will involve either a visit to San Salvador or at least travelling through it. Fortunately the country is so small that the capital can make a convenient base, thus avoiding the hassle of dragging your bags across the country.

Where to go

San Salvador is a cosmopolitan city with a variety of architectural styles that have been created by the multitude of rebuilding projects in a history dogged by earthquakes. The city centre is always busy and widely thought of as unsafe at night, so newcomers are best advised to head for the western areas around Boulevard de los Héroes, with its shopping malls and restaurants, and the residential districts of Escalón and the Zona Rosa with its major shopping malls – Multiplaza, Hipermall and La Gran Vía – with fancy stores, branded boutiques and a variety of restaurants and nightclubs.

Throughout El Salvador volcanoes dominate the landscape, and the scenery is one of its main attractions. Close to the capital, **Parque Balboa** affords fine views through the dramatic Puerta del Diablo (Devil's Door) and from the Mirador in the centre of the mountain village of **Los Planes de Renderos**. Below Los Planes de Renderos is **Panchimalco**, an old village where cultural traditions are kept alive by a growing handicraft industry. The community hosts the yearly Procesión de Las Palmas, a spectacular floral procession in the beginning of May. **Parque Nacional Cerro Verde**, just west of San Salvador, is a popular excursion for its prospect over Izalco and Santa Ana volcanoes and the deep-blue waters of the beautiful **Lago de Coatepeque**. Closed for two years after earthquakes, Cerro Verde recuperated its unique flora and fauna, was declared a protected natural area and is now open to foreign visitors. Also a short distance west of the capital are the country's main archaeological sites of **San Andrés** and the **Joya de Cerén**, where a Maya settlement has been preserved under volcanic ash. There are no grand temples and sculptures, but the dwellings and everyday objects found here are the only ones of their type preserved from the Maya era in Central America. Just north of San Salvador is **Cihuatán**, El Salvador's largest archaeological park and the largest city in Mesoamerica at the time of the Toltecs. The main city of the west is **Santa Ana**, which is also a good base for visiting the sites of **Tazumal** and **Casa Blanca** to the west.

A little further south, **Sonsonate** is an interesting town leading to the **Ruta de las Flores** a handful of villages climbing the volcanic chains with good scenery and waterfalls, pleasant hiking and a smattering of crafts.

There are very few pockets of undisturbed land, mainly because El Salvador is farmed intensively. On the border with Guatemala and Honduras is **Montecristo**, a remnant of cloud forest administered jointly by the three countries, while another such survivor is **Parque Nacional El Imposible**, one of the largest national parks in Central America. Just south of El Imposible is the **Barra de Santiago** protected natural area, home to a wide variety of species in the best preserved mangrove in the country.

North of San Salvador, near the Honduran border, are the towns of **La Palma** and **San Ignacio**, where handicrafts of brightly painted wood and other styles are made. Also

Don't miss ...

1 **Puerta del Diablo**, page 22.
2 **Ruta de las Flores**, page 34.
3 **Joya de Cerén**, page 36.
4 **Cerro Verde**, page 37.
5 **Suchitoto**, page 50.
6 **El Zonte, Tunco and Sunzal beaches**, pages 68 and 69.
7 **Parque Nacional El Imposible**, page 69.

Numbers relate to map on page 4.

north, but heading more to the east, is **Suchitoto**, one of the best preserved colonial towns, currently enjoying a revival that takes advantage of the beautiful scenery around Cerrón Grande resevoir. In eastern El Salvador are the cities of **San Vicente** and **San Miguel**, the port of **La Unión/Cutuco** and many small traditional towns. Those interested in the recent civil war can visit **Perquín**.

The Pacific coast at **La Libertad** is only a short trip from the capital and is a good place to start exploring the Balsam coast to the west, the surfing beaches and to get a feel for the country as a whole. The beaches of the **Costa del Sol** are definitely worth a stop for their long stretches of sand and estuaries. The **Gulf of Fonseca** has islands with secluded beaches which you can explore. In some parts of the country the infrastructure for tourism is quite rudimentary, but in others (such as the capital and nearby places of interest and some of the beach resorts) it is well developed.

Suggested itinerary

With so many crossings and borders, the options for travel in and around El Salvador are very flexible. Points of interest are spread throughout the country so there is no natural route to travel. If you want to visit **Parque Nacional El Imposible**, go for the La Hachadura crossing, drift through **Apaneca** and on to **San Salvador** before heading north to **Suchitoto**. If you're going to Honduras, head to **El Poy** if you want to drop into Santa Rosa de Copán or Gracias, or **Perquín** if you want Gracias or Tegucigalpa. For Nicaragua head to El Amatillo. El Salvador is subtly different to the other Central American nations. You could shoot through the main highlights in 10 days or else hang out for two to three weeks and soak up the nuances; if you've got the time, you'll enjoy the difference.

When to go

The most pleasant months are from November to January. El Salvador is fortunate in that temperatures are rarely excessively high. The average for San Salvador is 28°C with a variation of only about 3°C. March to May are the hottest months; December to February the coolest. There is one rainy season, from May to October, with April and November being transitional periods; there are only light rains for the rest of the year: the average annual rainfall is about 1830 mm. Highest temperatures and humidity will be found on the coast and in the lowlands, with the heat at its greatest from March to May.

What to do

El Salvador has been a popular **surfing** destination for several decades, from La Libertad heading west. Beyond this there is some diving in the coastal area and volcano lagoons.

National parks provide opportunities for **trekking** and **nature walks** in particular at Parque Nacional Cerro Verde close to San Salvador and in the more remote parks of Montecristo and Parque Nacional El Imposible.

Getting there

Air

From Europe To Miami with any transatlantic carrier, then to San Salvador with **American Airlines** or Taca. **Iberia** flies from Barcelona and Madrid via Miami.

The international airport is at Comalapa, 62 km southeast of San Salvador off the Coastal Highway, reached by a four-lane toll highway. There is a tourist information desk at the airport, which is open sporadically. If closed, you can still pick up some useful leaflets. Taxis and buses provide regular links to the capital. ▶▶ *See Transport, page 28.*

There is a 13% tax on international air tickets bought in El Salvador and an airport departure tax of US$32 for anyone staying more than six hours. The airport departure tax is now included in the ticket. The phone number for the airport authorities (**CEPA**) is T2339-9455. The airport has offices for all the main car rental companies and there are two banks, a tourist office and **Grupo Taca** and **American Airline** offices. Border formalities tend to be relatively brief although searches may be carried out.

From USA and Canada The main connection is with Miami. Other cities with flights to San Salvador are Atlanta, Dallas/Fort Worth, Houston, Los Angeles, Montreal, New Orleans, New York, Orlando, Phoenix, San Diego, San Francisco, Washington and Toronto.

From Central America and Mexico There are flights from all capitals and many larger cities in Mexico.

From South America Good connections to Colombia with a few flights to Barranquilla and Bogotá. Also connections with Buenos Aires, Cali, Caracas, Cartagena, Cucutá, Guayaquil, Quito, Lima, Medellín, Santa Marta and Santiago. Some flights go via San José or Panama City.

Road

Several border crossings with neighbouring countries. To the west the Pan-American Highway arrives from Guatemala at San Cristóbal through Santa Ana, Las Chinamas and La Hachadura, which is handy for Parque Nacional El Imposible. To the northwest the crossing is at Anguiatú. Also to the northwest the crossing at El Poy leads to southern Honduras, as does the crossing to the northeast at Perquín and to the east at El Amatillo.

Getting around

Road

Bus Bus services are good and cover most areas, although the buses are usually crowded. The best time to travel by bus is 0900-1500; avoid Friday and Sunday afternoons. All bus routes have a number, some also have a letter. Strange as it may seem, the system works and the route numbers don't change. Tickets are still unbelievably cheap, both within cities – usually around US$0.25 – and for long-distance journeys, which rarely cost more than US$1.50. Buses are brightly painted, particularly around San Miguel.

Transport is not difficult for the budget traveller as nearly all buses have luggage racks inside. For bigger bags there is sometimes space at the back where a couple of seats have been removed, so sit near there if you want to stay close to your bag. However, when problems on buses do occur they are usually at the back of the bus. The cheaper alternatives to the **Pullman** buses, which cross to Guatemala and Tegucigalpa from Puerto Bus Terminal in San Salvador, have luggage compartments beneath them and the luggage is tagged.

Taxi Apart from in the major cities taxis are rare, especially after dark. However, if you're eating out at night, you can usually arrange a lift at your hotel or restaurant for a small tip.

Car At the border, after producing a driving licence and proof of ownership, you are given a *comprobante de ingreso* (which has to be stamped by immigration, customs and quarantine), this is free of charge and you get the vehicle permit for 60 days. You need to have a passport from the same country as your driving licence or have an international licence and not have been in the country for more than 60 days. (If you are a foreigner residing in El Salvador you need to get a Salvadorean driver's licence.) You receive a receipt, vehicle permit and vehicle check document. Under no circumstances may the 60 days be extended, even though the driver may have been granted 90 days in the country. A few kilometres from the border the *comprobante* will be checked. When you leave the country a *comprobante de ingreso* must be stamped again and, if you don't intend to return, your permit must be surrendered. Do not overstay your permitted time unless you wish to be fined. Leaving the country for a few days in order to return for a new permit is not recommended as customs officials are wise to this and may fine you anyway. To bring a vehicle in permanently involves a complex procedure costing thousands of dollars.

Petrol costs per US gallon US$3.60 (super), US$3.20 (regular), US$2.80 (diesel), though as everywhere, prices are constantly rising. All fuel is unleaded. **Roads** are very good throughout the country, but look out for crops being dried at the roadside or in central reservations. Take care of buses, which travel very fast. Third-party, **insurance** is compulsory in El Salvador and can be arranged at the border (enquire first at consulates). Under the 1996 law, **seat belts** must be worn; the fine for not doing so is US$57. The fine for **drink-driving** is US$57. If your alcohol level is very high you go straight to jail and have to await the sentence. Do not attempt to bribe the officials. For more information, call **Ministerio de Transporte** ① *T2281-0678 0679*.

Sleeping and eating price codes

Sleeping

$$$$	over US$150	**$$$**	US$66-150
$$	US$30-65	**$**	under US$30

Price codes refer to a standard double/twin room in high season.

Eating

$$$	over US$15	**$$**	US$8-15	**$**	under US$8

Price codes refer to the cost of a two-course meal, not including drinks.

Sleeping

As the most industrialized of the Central American states El Salvador has an impressive selection of international-standard business hotels in San Salvador. The country also has a good selection of more expensive hotels for those taking weekend breaks from the capital. At the lower end there is no shortage of cheap accommodation, but there is a shortage of good, cheap accommodation. If you have the time, shop around, don't check into the first hotel you come to. If travelling at holiday times book accommodation in advance. **Ximena's Guest House** off Boulevard de Los Héroes is recognized as a hotel where backpackers meet up.

Eating and drinking

Pupusas, stuffed tortillas made of corn or ricemeal, are the quintessential Salvadorean dish. They come in several varieties including *chicharrón* (pork crackling), *queso* (cheese) and *revueltas* (mixed), and are typical, tasty and cheap. The ones sold at street stalls are better there than at restaurants, but beware stomach infection from the accompanying *curtido* (pickled cabbage). On Saturday and Sunday nights people congregate in *pupuserías*. *Pavo* (turkey) is common and good, as are *frijoles* (red beans). A *boca* is an appetizer, a small dish of yucca, avocado or chorizo, served with a drink before a meal. Apart from in San Salvador, restaurants tend to close early, around 2000.

    Coffee makes an excellent souvenir and is good value and delicious.

    Beer Light lagers are the norm, as elsewhere in Central America; Suprema is stronger than Pilsener, while Golden Light is a reduced-alcohol beer.

    Chicha is a traditional alcoholic drink made from corn, sometimes with a trace of pineapple; El Salvador also has a stronger, distilled version called *chaparro*. Although illegal to sell, everyone has their source. When made well *chicha* can taste similar to white wine. It is a trademark of the Maya and is particularly well made in the western village of Izalco. Ask at the tourist office there for a *chicha* contact to purchase a sample. *Chaparro curado* contains fruit or honey. It is a favourite at election times when alcohol sales are banned. Water bottles are emptied and filled with the clear *chaparro* for illegal swigging on the streets.

Festivals and events

1 Jan New Year's Day.
Mar/Apr Holy Week (3 days,
government 10 days).
1 May Labour Day.
10 May Mothers' Day.
First week of Aug Corpus Christi (half day).
15 Sep (half day).

2 and **5 Nov** (half day).
24 Dec (half day) and **Christmas Day**.
Government offices are also closed on
religious holidays. Look in newspapers
for details of regional fiestas and other fairs.
There are many craft fairs, for example at
San Sebastián and **San Vicente**.

Shopping

The best place to buy arts and crafts is in the village where the items are originally made;
Ilobasco for ceramics, **San Sebastián** for hammocks and **La Palma** for painted wooden
boxes, **Nahuizalco** for baskets and furniture of wicker and jute. If you cannot go there in
person, the markets in **San Salvador** (Mercado Ex-Cuartel and Mercado de Artesanía) sell
many of these items at a slightly higher prices. Branches of Nahanché have outlets in the
major shopping malls with good quality handicrafts from all over the country.

Essentials A-Z

Accident and emergency
Police: 911; **Fire service**: T2527-7300; **Red Cross**: T2222-5155; **Hospitals**: T2225-4481; **Public hospital**: Rosales T2231-9200; **Public maternity**: Hospital de Maternidad T2529-8200; **Private Hospital Pro Familia**: T2244-8000; **Private Maternity**: T2271-2555; **Hospital Ginecológico**: T2247-1122.

Customs and duty free
All personal luggage is allowed in free. Also permitted: 50 cigars or 200 cigarettes, and 2 litres of liquor, 2 used cameras or a video recorder, 1 personal stereo, 1 portable computer and new goods up to US$1000 in value (best to have receipts). No restrictions on the import of foreign currency; up to the amount imported and declared may also be exported. Check with www.aduana.gob.sv for full information.

Phone numbers for Salvadorean border crossings: **Hachadura**: T2420-3767, Chinamas: T2401-3601; **San Cristóbal**: T2441-8109; **El Poy**: T2335-9401; **Angiatú**: T2401-0231; **Amatillo**: T2649-9388.

Electricity
110 volts, 60 cycles, AC (US-style flat-pin plugs). Supply is far from stable; important electrical equipment should have surge protectors.

Embassies and consulates
For more countries, visit www.rree.gob.sv.
Belgium, Av de Tervuren 171, 2nd floor, 1150 Brussels, T733-0485.
Canada, 209 Kent St K2P 1Z8, Ottawa, Ontario, T613-238-2939, also in Montreal and Vancouver.
Germany, Joachin-Karnatz-Allee 47, 10557, Berlín (Tiergarten), T30-206-4660, www.botschaft-elsalvador.de.
Israel, 4 Avigail, Apto 4, Abu-Tor, Jerusalem, Israel. 93551, T267-28411.

Italy, Via Gualtiero Castellini 13, Scala B int, 3, 00197 Roma, T06-807-6605.
Japan, Kowa 38, Building 803, Nishi Azabu 4 Ch, Tokyo, Japan 106, T33499-4461.
Spain, Calle Serrano 114, 2 Edif Izquierda, 28006 Madrid, T91-562-8002.
Mexico, Calle Temístocles 88 Col Polanco, México DF, T5281-5725.
UK, 2nd floor, 8 Dorset Sq, London, NW1 6PU, T020-7224-9800.
US: 1400 Sixteenth NW Washington, DC 20036, T202-387-6511; with consulates in several other large cities.

Health
Gastroenteritic diseases are most common. Visitors should take care over what they eat during the first few weeks, and should drink *agua cristal* (purified bottled water). The bags of water sold in the street are not always safe and taste somewhat of rubber. Cases of dengue are rare in adults. For diarrhoea, mild dysentery, amoebas and parasitic infections get *Nodik* tablets from any chemist or large supermarket, approx US$14 for a 3-day cure. El Salvador has one of the best health systems in Central America, so the capital is a good place to sort out problems. You can get a stool sample taken at the **Pro-Familia Hospital**, 25 Av Norte, near Metro Centro, which gives you the result in about 6-12 hrs.

Internet
Internet cafés are widespread in the capital and are now commonplace in smaller places outside San Salvador. Most hotels will offer both internet service and wireless connection.

Language
Spanish is the official language and English is widely understood in business and travel industry-related circles. See page 88 for Spanish words and phrases.

Money → *US$1=8.75 colones (fixed).*
El Salvador adopted the dollar on 1 Jan 2001 and the national currency – the colón – is now totally replaced. All US coinage and notes are widely used, although you may have problems with US$20 bills and above. There are some small shops and street merchants that still price their products in colones, but they are in the minority.

ATMs and exchange
Do not find yourself in the countryside without cash or credit cards; traveller's cheques (TCs) are of limited use outside the capital and major cities. You can use credit cards in pretty much any store (except small *tiendas*). See under San Salvador, Banks, page 30, regarding exchange of TCs. Be aware that some banks will want to see your original purchase receipt. Credit cards are widely accepted and are charged at the official rate. There are international Visa and MasterCard ATMs in El Salvador and larger cities throughout the country. For cash advances on Visa or MasterCard, go to **Aval-Visa** or **Banco de América Central de El Salvador**.

All ATMs and banks give US dollars in cash (so no need for exchange). Pretty much all gas stations have ATMs.

Cost of living and travelling
El Salvador is reasonably priced and 2 people should be able to travel for US$40 per person per day. However, the range of services open to the foreign tourist is still limited (although growing) so the quality of hotels is not as good as that offered in neighbouring countries for the same price.

Opening hours
Banks Mon-Fri 0900-1700, Sat 0900-1200, closed between 29-30 Jun and 30-31 Dec.
Businesses Mon-Fri 0800-1200, 1400-1730; Sat 0800-1200.
Government offices Mon-Fri 0730-1530.

Post
Airmail to and from Europe can take up to a month, but is normally about 15 days; from the USA, 1 week. Certified packets to Europe cost US$9.25 per kilo and regular service is US$8.50 per kilo, good service; swifter, but more expensive, is **EMS** (US$34 per kg to Europe). Courier services are much quicker, but cost more. The correct address for any letter to the capital is 'San Salvador, El Salvador, Central America'.

Safety
Traditionally El Salvador has a reputation for violence and crime. In part this is a legacy of many years of civil war although this has been improved through a more active role of the police in later years. The reality is that most people visiting El Salvador return with reports of friendly, open people; far from being targeted by criminals, you are much more likely to receive a warm welcome and genuine interest in your visit. Locals will talk incessantly about the country's problems and dangers but few actual examples materialize. Be cautious until you find your own level of comfort and always ask local advice. Statistically El Salvador has the unenviable distinction of having the worst levels of violent crime on the continent. This derives from Salvadorean gang culture (*maras*) and most visitors will see nothing of this activity. If renting a car, buy a steering lock. Visitors to San Salvador should seek advice on where is not safe both inside and outside the city.

Telephone → *Country code T+503.*
The **international direct dialling** code (to call out of El Salvador) is T00; 144+00 for **Telefónica**. There are no local area codes within El Salvador. There is a network of public phones for telecommunications companies – all use prepaid phone cards that only work in the company's particular machines. Available at most street corners,

supermarkets, gas stations to small stores they can be used for local and international calls, but make sure the card is from the same company as the public phone. The cards come in several denominations (US$1-3, US$5, US$10, US$25, etc). Mobile phones are very cheap. You can get a SIM card for US$3 and if you need a mobile phone you can get one fromas little as US$12.

Some hotels will provide direct dialling – by far the easiest option. Dial T114 for **Information** (English spoken) and details of phone numbers in capital.

Time
- 6 hrs GMT.

Tipping
In upmarket restaurants: 10%, in others, give small change. Check your bill as most now add the 10% at the end (if they have, an additional tip is not needed). Nothing for taxi drivers except when hired for the day; airport porters, *boinas rojas* (red berets), US$2 per bag.

Tourist information
Corporación Salvadoreña de Turismo (**Corsatur**), at the Ministry of Tourism, Edificio Carbonel No1, Col Roma Alameda Dr Manuel Enrique Araujo Pasaje Carbonel San Salvador, T2243-7835; T2241-3200, www.elsalvador.travel. Provides information locally and on the web.
Revue, www.revuemag.com. English-language magazine published in Guatemala, with a section on El Salvador. Contains articles on places to visit and details of activities.

Useful websites
www.alfatravelguide.com Has a comprehensive listings of hotels throughout the country.
www.elsalvador.com Site of *El Diario de Hoy* – look in 'Otros Sitios' for tourist info.

www.diariocolatino.com Site of the leftist *Co Latino* newspaper.
www.laprensa.com.sv Site of *La Prensa Gráfica* newspaper.
www.mipatria.net and **www.theother elsalvador.com** Access to useful information.
www.turismo.com.sv Lists of hotels, restaurants and interesting places to visit.
www.utec.edu.sv Site of Centre for Investigation of El Salvadorean Public Opinion (CIOPS) with information in Spanish on El Salvadorean political and social issues.

Visas and immigration
Every visitor must have a valid passport. No visas are required for European, US, Canadian, Australian or New Zealand nationals. The government website www.rree.gob.sv has a full list of country requirements.

Overstaying the limit on a tourist card can result in fines. Immigration officials can authorize up to 90 days stay in the country; extensions may be permitted on application to Migración, Centro de Gobierno (see under San Salvador). As of 2006, when El Salvador signed a Central America-4 (CA-4) Border Control Agreement with Guatemala, Honduras, and Nicaragua, you have to visit a country outside of these 4 to re-enter and gain 90 days. Travel between these 4 countries now involves minimal customs control: no entry stamp in your passport, only an exit stamp from departing country. Nevertheless, always check at a Salvadorean consulate for any changes to the rules.

Weights and measures
The metric system is used alongside certain local units such as the *vara* (836 mm), *manzana* (7000 sq m) and the *quintal* (45 kg). Some US weights and measures are also used; US gallons are used for gasoline and quarts for oil.

Contents

Footprint features

El Salvador

At a glance

◉ **Getting around** Buses are efficient and economical.

◔ **Time required** 2-3 weeks would be best if you have the time.

❦ **Weather** High 20°Cs throughout the year, with most rainfall May-Oct.

✖ **When not to go** The wettest weather and highest temperatures are in May, when it's hot and humid.

San Salvador

Surrounded by a ring of mountains in a valley known as 'Valle de las Hamacas', San Salvador has suffered from both natural and man-made disasters. El Salvador's capital is a bustling cosmopolitan city with a rich blend of architectural styles; modern, yet retaining the charm of the Spanish era with the privilege of being one of the first European cities in the New World. Today, crumbling buildings await renovation and restoration, or the arrival of the next earthquake to deliver the final death knell. As always, some areas speed to recovery, and the shopping malls and wealthy suburbs to the west stand out in the pollution-filled valley. The further northwest you get from the city centre the higher you climb and the cleaner the air becomes.

San Salvador itself does not have many natural attractions, but there are several day trips to nearby volcanoes, crater lakes and beauty spots such as Los Planes de Renderos, the Puerto del Diablo and San Salvador's own volcano, Boquerón, which has a paved road all the way to the top. There are, surprisingly, many green areas and trees planted alongside the streets giving the city a refreshing atmosphere. If you spend a few days in the city and surrounding area you could be pleasantly surprised by how easy it is to get around and how much there is to do.

Ins and outs → *Altitude: 680-1000 m. Population: 2,297,282 including suburbs).*
Getting there The **international airport** (SAL) is at Comalapa, 62 km southeast of San Salvador towards Costa del Sol beach, reached by a four-lane, toll highway. Some domestic flights use the old airport at Ilopango, 13 km east of the capital. Most **international buses** arrive at the Puerto Bus terminal, although luxury services and Ticabus have their own terminals. Domestic bus lines use terminals at the east, south and west ends of the city. ►► *See Transport, page 28.*

Getting around The main focal points of the city are the historical centre, the commercial district some 3 km to the west around Boulevard de los Héroes, and the residential and commercial districts of Escalón and Zona Rosa another 2 km further west. City buses and taxis are needed to get between the three (see page 28).

Four broad streets meet at the centre: Avenida Cuscatlán and its continuation Avenida España run south to north; Calle Delgado and its continuation Calle Arce, with a slight blip, from east to west. This principle is retained throughout: the *avenidas* run north to south and the *calles* east to west. The even-numbered *avenidas* are east of the central *avenidas*, odd numbers west; north of the central *calles*, they are dubbed Norte, south of the central *calles* Sur. The even-numbered *calles* are south of the two central *calles*, the odd numbers north. East of the central *avenidas* they are dubbed Oriente (Ote), west of the central *avenidas* Poniente (Pte). Sounding more complicated than it is, the system is straightforward and quickly grasped.

Tourist information Corporación Salvadoreña de Turismo (Corsatur) ① *Edif Carbonel No 1, Col Roma Alameda Dr Manuel Enrique Araujo Pasaje Carbonel San Salvador, T2243-7835, www.elsalvador.travel, Mon-Fri 0800-1230, 1330-1730*. Good information on buses, archaeological sites, beaches and national parks. Texaco and Esso sell good maps at some of their service stations. The best maps of the city and country are available from the **Instituto Geográfico Nacional** ① *1 Calle Pte y 43 Av Norte 02310, Col Flor Blanca, T2260-8000*. The **Instituto Salvadoreño de Turismo (ISTU)** ① *Calle Rubén Darío 619, San Salvador Centre, T2222-8000*, has useful information about the 13 government-run **Turicentros** recreation and water parks in the country and on Cerro Verde and Walter T Deininger national parks.

Best time to visit The climate is semi-tropical and healthy, and the water supply relatively pure. Days are often hot, especially in the dry season, but the temperature drops in the late afternoon and nights are usually pleasantly mild. Since it is in a hollow, the city has a very bad smog problem, caused mainly by traffic pollution. Efforts are being made to reduce vehicle emissions.

Safety The city centre is considered by many to be dangerous after dark, but the area north of Bulevar de los Héroes up to around San Antonio Abad is quite safe. As a general rule, stay out of poorly lit areas and keep to main roads where there are more people around. At night, taxis are a sensible alternative if you don't know where you're going exactly.

Armed security personnel are commonplace. There is a heightened atmosphere of tension in some areas. In downtown markets, don't carry cameras, don't wear watches or jewellery and don't flash money around.

Sights → *For listings, see pages 24-32.*

A number of important buildings are near the intersection of the main roads in the historic centre. On the east side of Avenida Cuscatlán is the **Plaza Barrios**, the heart of the city. A fine equestrian statue looks west towards the renaissance-style **Palacio Nacional** (1904-1911). To the north is the **New Cathedral**, which was left unfinished for several years after Archbishop Romero suspended its construction to use the money to reduce poverty. Work was resumed in 1990 and completed in 1999, the last consecration of a cathedral of the millennium. It now stands as a beacon of tranquillity amid the dirt and noise of the downtown capital. It commands a striking presence, gleaming white and modern, its façade flanked by two giant murals vividly splashed with the colourful work of the country's most famous artist, **Fernando Llort**. Inside it is quite bare, but for the fabulous circular stained-glass window of a dove surrounded by a hundred shards of brilliant yellow glass, which in turn is framed by yellow stars set in deep lapis lazuli-blue glass. Beneath the cathedral, a new chapel has been created to house the tomb of assassinated **Archbishop Oscar Romero**.

East of Plaza Barrios, on Calle Delgado, is the **Teatro Nacional**, whose interior has been magnificently restored. If you walk along 2 Calle Oriente you pass, on the right, **Parque Libertad** with the rebuilt church of **El Rosario** on the eastern side where José Matías Delgado, father of the Independence movement, lies buried. The interior, decked out in modern sculpture, is fascinating; go early morning or late afternoon to see the stunning light effect of the modern stained-glass window. The **Palacio Arquiepiscopal** is

① San Salvador

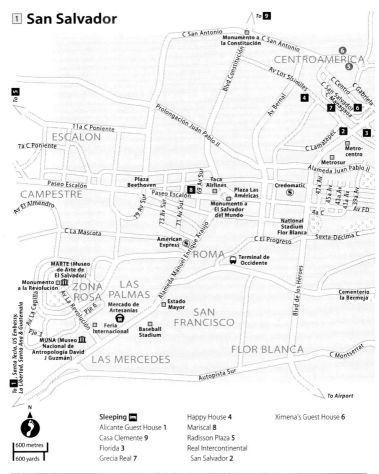

next door. Not far away to the southeast, on 10 Avenida Sur, is another rebuilt church, **La Merced**, whose belltower rang out Father Delgado's tocsin call to Independence in 1811.

One block north, across Calle Delgado, is the **Teatro Nacional** ① *Plaza Morazán, T2222-5689*, with a monument to General Morazán. The theatre reopened in 2008, after a complete restoration following earthquake damage in 2001; it hosts a regular programme of performances, sometimes free, in a sumptuous auditorium with red velvet seats. Heading east along Delgado is the **Mercado Ex-Cuartel**, and the expected confusion of sounds and smells that besiege the senses. Nearby are some of the cheapest hotels in the city. Running west from the Teatro Nacional, Calle Arce leads to **Hospital**

Bars & clubs 🎵
Café La 7 **5**
El Arpa (Bar Irlandés) **6**
La Luna **3**

Rosales and its own gardens. On the way to the hospital is the great church of **El Sagrado Corazón de Jesús**, which is well worth a visit; don't miss the stained-glass windows. Turn left (south) here and after one block you come to the **Parque Bolívar**, with the national printing office to the south and the Department of Health to the north.

Four streets north of Calle Arce is the Alameda Juan Pablo II, an important road for bus transport, on which stands **Parque Infantil**, where you will find the Palacio de los Deportes. One block west is the **Centro de Gobierno**, with many official buildings.

The north side of Parque Bolívar is Calle Rubén Darío (2 Calle Poniente), which becomes Alameda Roosevelt, then Paseo General Escalón as it runs through the commercial and residential districts west of the centre. Heading west this boulevard first passes **Parque Cuscatlán**. A major junction is with 49 Avenida: to the south this avenue soon passes the national stadium, **Estadio Olímpico Flor Blanca**, before becoming the main highway to the international airport. To the north, 49 Avenida crosses Alameda Juan Pablo II beyond which it changes name to **Bulevar de los Héroes**, home to the fashionable shopping centres, **Metrocentro** and the newer **Metrosur**, the **Hotel Real Intercontinental**, some of the city's better restaurants and a glut of fast-food places, which is a busy area at all times, especially at night. At the Shell station by Metrocentro,

② **San Salvador centre**

Sleeping ▭
American Guest House **1**   El Palacio **3**
Centro Histórico **2**

mariachis and other musicians gather each evening, waiting to be hired; others wander around the restaurants, playing to diners.

Continuing west along Alameda Roosevelt, the next landmark at the Plaza Las Américas is the **Monumento al Salvador del Mundo**, a statue of Jesus standing on the Earth atop a column. From this junction the Pan-American Highway heads southwest to **Santa Tecla**. Straight ahead is Paseo General Escalón, Parque Beethoven and an area with many restaurants, shops and the Colonia Escalón residential district. Hidden behind the towering office blocks flanking the monument is the **Museo Forma** ① *Av Manuel Enrique Araujo, T2298-4269, www.fjuliadiaz.org, Mon-Fri 0900-1700, Sat 0900-1200, US$1.50*, a small modern art gallery housed in a neocolonial-style castle, with an interesting collection of paintings and sculpture by Salvadorean artists.

Another important residential and entertainment region is the **Zona Rosa** and **Colonia San Benito**, reached either from the Pan-American Highway or from Escalón. In this leafy suburb, some of the most elegant restaurants and the **Hotel Sheraton Presidente** and **Hotel Hilton Princess** (where former US president Clinton stayed while on his Central America tour) are found. **MUNA (Museo Nacional de Antropología David J Guzmán)** ① *Feria Internacional, Av de la Revolución y Carretera a Santa Tecla, T2243-3750, Tue-Sun 0900-1700, US$3*, is a modern museum worth visiting, showcasing exhibits on the country's archaeological and historical past as well as numerous cultural events; descriptions in Spanish only, but free guided tours available in afternoons with English-speaking guides (check at desk as they only operate if enough visitors). Just north of the museum at the end of Avenida Revolución is **MARTE (Museo de Arte de El Salvador)** ① *T2243-6099, Tue-Sun 1000-1800, US$1.50 (free on Sun), café and shop (both closed Sun) in lobby*. This privately run modern arts museum has permanent exhibits depicting the history of Salvadorean painters with temporary exhibits of artists from Latin America and other parts of the world.

A little further north is **El Arbol de Dios** ① *La Mascota y Av Masferrer, T2224-6200, Mon-Sat 1000-2200*, an arts and crafts store, restaurant, museum and garden, operated by the famed Salvadorean artist Fernando Llort, who designed the façade of the Metropolitan Cathedral and is known for his naïf-style wood paintings. The display here also includes the work of other artists.

In Colonia San Benito is **Museo de Ciencias Físicas Stephen Hawking** ① *Av*

➡ San Salvador maps
1 San Salvador, page 18
2 San Salvador centre, page 20

Reforma 179, T2223-3027, Mon-Sat 1000-1400, US$1.25, with sections on astronomy, ecology, electronics and biochemistry. Interactive exhibits about the sciences with monthly lectures on scientific topics. This area also has many art galleries such as *Galería Espacio I Av La Capilla, Galería 1-2-3 I Calle La Reforma, La Pinacoteca I Blv Hipódromo,* to name a few. See local press for details.

Worth visiting is the **María Auxiliadora church**, locally known as 'don Rua', situated in Barrio San Miguelito. This multi-coloured marble temple – a copy of the cathedral in Turin (Italy) – is one of the city's landmarks, displaying a Venetian clock tower and with a spectacular view from the belltower.

Museo Militar de las Fuerzas Armadas ① *behind the presidential palace of San Jacinto at the former Cuartel El Zapote,* has a collection of exhibits of weapons, uniforms and decorations of the armed forces, and weapons captured from FMLN guerrillas. **Mercado de San Miguelito** is an indoor market located close to don Rua. Safer than many of the other city markets and famous for its *comedores* which offer typical Salvadorean dishes (difficult to find outside a traditional Salvadorean home) at economic prices. There are several food stalls throughout the place – look for the area dedicated just to *comedores* at the far end of the market. It's a great place to watch people go about their shopping and to enjoy the display of stalls.

A good sightseeing tour of the surrounding area heads south to a couple of local places of interest. Lasting most of the day by bus (No 12) or two to three hours by car it starts a few blocks southwest of the main square on the eastern side of the Mercado Central. It includes the **San Salvador Zoo** ① *T2270-0828, Wed-Sun 0900-1600, US$0.60,* which, although small, is quiet and attractive. Just three blocks away is the **Museo de Historia Natural** ① *Parque Saburo Hirao,* with interesting displays on prehistoric findings and a herbal medicine garden. To get there, take bus No 2 ' Zoo', and No 12 from the centre. You then pass the **Casa Presidencial** and go on up to the residential district in the mountain range of **Planes de Renderos**. This place is crowned by the beautiful **Parque Balboa** ① *daily 0800-1800,* and there's a good view of the city from El Mirador at the foot of the park. Parque Balboa is a **Turicentro**, with cycle paths, playground and gardens. From the park a scenic road runs to the summit of **Cerro Chulo**, from which the view, seen through the Puerta del Diablo (Devil's Door), is even better. There are local buses to Puerta del Diablo and Parque Balboa (No 12 from eastern side of Mercado Central and No 12-MC marked 'Mil Cumbres') almost hourly. Bus No 17 goes from the same location to Panchimalco through Los Planes de Renderos so you can get off at the junction there and take the No 12 to Parque Balboa and Puerta del Diablo.

The **Puerta del Diablo** consists of two enormous, nearly vertical rocks which frame a magnificent view of the Volcán San Vicente. The rocks are very steep but the sides can be climbed on reasonable paths for an even better view. A little beyond the car park and drinks stands at the Puerta del Diablo is a path climbing up a further summit, from which there are 360° views: to the coast, Lago Ilopango, the capital and volcanoes, including San Salvador, Izalco and Cerro Verde and San Vicente.

At the foot of Cerro Chulo is **Panchimalco** (see below). The route to Panchimalco (No 17 from Mercado Central) and the coast branches off the road to Parque Balboa at the village of **Los Planes**, a few kilometres before the park.

Around San Salvador

Many places can be visited in a day from San Salvador either on the frequent bus services or by car. To the south is the indigenous village of **Panchimalco**, heading east are the beautiful setting and views around **Lago de Ilopango**; and to the southwest the crater of **Volcán San Salvador** (see Santa Tecla, page 36).

Heading west towards Santa Ana, but still manageable in a day, are the archaeological sites of **Joyo de Cerén**, El Salvador's Pompeii, and **San Andrés** and the peaks of **Volcán Izalco** and **Cerro Verde** (see page 37) with the deep blue waters of **Lago de Coatepeque** in the crater below. The limits of a comfortable weekend trip will take you to the garden park of **Ichanmichen**, which is restful (see page 71), and the pyramid of **Tazumal** (west of Santa Ana) is also worth a visit (see page 38). At weekends the coast around La Libertad (see page 67) is very popular. Bus 495 from the Terminal del Occidente goes to the seaside resort of **Costa del Sol** (see page 70).

Panchimalco

This small town and the surrounding area is home to the Pancho, descendants of the Pipil tribes, one of the region's dominant indigenous groups prior to conquest. This is one of the few places in El Salvador where you can still see indigenous people in traditional dress. Streets of large cobbles, with low adobe houses, thread their way between huge boulders at the foot of Cerro Chulo. A very fine baroque colonial church, Santa Cruz, has a white façade with statues of eight saints. Inside are splendid woodcarvings and wooden columns, altars, ceilings and benches. There is a bell inscribed with the cipher and titles of the Holy Roman Emperor Charles V, and a colourful cemetery. The Casa de La Cultura in the main street has frequent cultural events and crafts stores. The **Fiesta de Santa Cruz de Roma** is held on 12-14 September, with music and traditional dances; on 3 May (or the second Sunday of the month) there is the procession of **Las Palmas**. Bus 17 from Mercado Central at 12 Calle Poniente, San Salvador, every 45 minutes (45 minutes), or minibus from near Mercado Central, very crowded but quicker (30 minutes), and cheaper (US$0.80).

Lago de Ilopango

Beyond the four-lane highway to Ilopango airport (14.5 km east) lie the deep waters of Lago de Ilopango. Surrounded by mountains, the views around El Salvador's largest and deepest crater lake are impressive. Before the conquest local people used to appease the harvest gods by drowning four virgins here every year. Private chalets make access to the lake difficult, except at clubs and the **Turicentro Apulo**, but it is well worth a visit. The eastern shore is less polluted and is reached from Cojutepeque. There are a number of lakeside cafés and bathing clubs, some of which hire dug-outs by the hour. The cafés are busy in the dry season (try **Teresa's** for fish dishes), but often closed in the middle of the year. **Hotel Vista del Lago** ① *3 km from Apulo turn-off on the highway*, is on a hill top. Bus 15, marked Apulo, runs from the bus stop on Parque Hula Hula to the lake (via the airport), 1¼ hours, US$1. Entrance to the Turicentro **camping site** costs US$0.60.

Volcán San Salvador

This large massif at 1839 m has an impressive crater, more than 1.5 km wide and 543 m deep, known as **El Boquerón**. About 2 km to the east is the equally dramatic peak of **El Picacho** (1960 m), which dominates the capital. Buses leave a block from Plaza Merliot. By car you turn right just after the Plaza Merliot Mall and continue to the end of the road where a paved road take you up the volcano. A walk clockwise round the crater takes about two hours; the first half is easy, the second half rough. The views are magnificent, if somewhat spoilt by TV and radio towers. The area by Boquerón is now a park administrated by the Ministry of Tourism. The area is closed off, with guards during opening hours (daily 0800-1500). **La Laguna** botanical garden is near the summit. The inner slopes of the crater are covered with trees, and at the bottom is a smaller cone from the eruption of 1917.

You can follow the road north and then turn right through extensive coffee plantations and forest to reach the summit of **El Picacho**. This also makes an excellent climb from the Escalón suburb of San Salvador, in the early morning preferably, which takes about three to four hours return trip (take a guide). The easy access, great views and fresh climate has made the Volcano of San Salvador a popular destination for people in the capital and, as a result, new restaurants have opened their doors in recent years. See Eating, page 25. Another access to the volcano from the city side is by **Ecoparque El Espino** ① *run by El Espino Cooperative T2289-0749/69 www.ecoparqueelespino.com, US$1.50*. The entrance is by the Polideportivo in Ciudad Merliot, take bus No 42 C especial and walk 100 m. They have several trails, bike rental and small cafeterias. The trails end at a mirador with a panoramic view of the city.

San Salvador listings

For Sleeping and Eating price codes and other relevant information, see page 10.

⊜ Sleeping

San Salvador *p16, maps p18 and p20*
In the downtown area, some hotels lock their doors very early. Many cheap *hospedajes* near **Terminal de Oriente** are of dubious safety and not recommended for single women. Foreigners are advised not to be out in the city centre after dark.

13% VAT (IVA) is added to bills at major hotels. Most of the cheaper hotels are around the Centro Histórico. Be careful in this area, particularly at night.
$$$$ Hotel Real Intercontinental San Salvador, Blv de los Héroes and Av Sisimiles, in front of the Metrocentro, T2211-3333, www.grupo real.com. A useful landmark, smart, formal atmosphere (popular with business

visitors), **Avis** car hire, **Taca** desk, shop selling souvenirs, postcards, US papers and magazines.
$$$ Radisson Plaza, 89 Av Norte and 11 Calle Pte, Col Escalón, T2257-0700, www.radisson.com. Elegant rooms with a/c and cable TV. Good value, with parking.
$$ Alicante Guest House, Calle las Rosas y Av Los Laureles 1, Col La Sultana, T2243-0889, www.alicante.com.sv. Telephone, cable TV, restaurant, internet access for guests, breakfast included. Discounts for extended stays.
$$ Grecia Real, Av Sisimiles 2922, Col Miramontes, 50 m west of **Hotel Real Intercontinental**, T2261-0555, www.greciareal.com. With good Greek restaurant. Recommended.
$$ Happy House, Av Sisimiles 2951, Col Miramonte, T2260-1568, www.hotel happyhouse-elsalvador.com. Good, friendly, parking, good breakfast.

$$ Mariscal, Paseo Escalón 3658, T2283-0220, www.hotelmariscal.com. Good apartments, a good deal for long-term stay.

$ American Guest House, 17 Av Norte 119 between Calle Arce y 1 Calle Pte, 3 blocks from Puerto Bus, T2222-8789. With bath (cheaper without), hot water, fan, helpful, will store luggage, accepts credit cards, discounts for groups. Oldest guest house downtown, run by the young at heart Irma Estradain her 70s, weekly rates, **Cafetería La Amistad**, parking nearby, good.

$ Casa Clementina, Av Morazán y Av Washington 34, Col Libertad, T2225-5962. Very friendly, clean, pleasant, garden.

$ Centro, 9 Av Sur 410, T2271-5045, hotel_centro55@hotmail.com. A bit box-like, check out 1200, cable TV, internet, TV, phone, friendly, washing facilities, clean, safe. Recommended.

$ Centro Histórico, 1 Calle Pte 124 y 1 Av Norte, 2 blocks from cathedral, T2221-5086, www.hotelescentrohistorico.com.sv. A/c, TV, parking, good choice.

$ Hospedaje España, 12 Av Norte 123, T2222-5248. Fan, clean, bright, good value.

$ Hotel Florida, Pasaje Los Almendros 15, Urbanización Florida and Blv de los Héroes, T2260-2540. All rooms with bath, fan, laundry service, some with a/c, thin walls but good value, secure. Recommended.

$ Nuevo Panamericano, 8 Av Sur 113, T2222-2959. Cold shower, safe, open 24 hrs, parking. Recommended.

$ Ximena's Guest House, Calle San Salvador 202, Col Centroamérica, T2260-2481, www.ximenasguesthouse.com. A variety of rooms with private bath and hot shower, cheaper in 6-bed dormitory. Wi-Fi. Friendly and knowledgeable staff (ask for Lena, speaks several languages). Variety of economic tours as well as transport to their beach house **Capricho** and **Lisa Guest House** at organic farm. Conveniently located, but not easy to find (behind the Esso station on Blv de los Héroes). Recommended.

🍴 Eating

San Salvador *p16, maps p18 and p20*
In the older downtown area few places are open to eat after 1830. Restaurants are open later in the western sections of the city. Along Blv Hipódromo, San Benito, restaurants are generally very good, but expensive. On Blv de los Héroes there are many restaurants, including US-style fast-food places. The strip along Calle San Antonio Abad has several local eateries.

$$$ Al Pomodoro, Paseo Escalón 3952, Col Escalón, T2257-2544, www.alpomodoro.com. Popular, good Italian, also does delivery.

$$$ Dynasty, Blv Hipódromo 738-B, T2263-9955. Known for serving the best Chinese food in the city.

$$$ El Bodegón, Paseo Escalón 3956 and 77 Av Norte, T2263-5283. The proprietor is Spanish, as is the food. Excellent.

$$$ H'ola Beto's Escalón, Pasaje Dordelly 4352 between 85 and 87 Av Norte (above Paseo Escalón). Best seafood in the city, also serves Italian. Great service, parking. Recommended.

$$$ Kamakura, 93 Av Norte 617, Col Escalón T2263-2401. Japanese food.

$$$ La Hacienda Real, just opposite of La Gran Vía Mall T, Km 8, Carretera Panamericana, next to Air Force offices, T2243-8567. Without a doubt the best steaks in El Salvador, excellent service and finger-licking food.

$$$ La Panetière, Plaza Villavicencio, local 5, Paseo Escalón. Delicious French pastry, crêpes, cappuccinos, popular with foreigners, a bit pricey but worth it.

$$ Automariscos, located next to roundabout by the Don Rua church, 5a Av Norte, Blv Tutunichapa, T2226-5363, also outlet in San Benito, Av Revolución No 179 (between Pizza Hut and Anthropological museum), T2243-3653. Out-of-the-ordinary seafood and huge portions. Recommended.

$$ Café Café, Calle El Tanque, 99 Av Norte y 7 y 9 Calle Pte bis 130, T2263-4034, www.cafe

cafe.com.sv. Locally popular Peruvian restaurant. Recommended.

$$ El Sopón Típico, 71 Av Norte and 1 Calle Pte 3702, Col Escalón, T2298-3008 and Blv de Los Héroes, Pasaje Las Palmeras 130, Urb Florida T2260-2671, www.elsopontipico.com. Typical Salvadorean soups and other dishes, including *gallo en chicha* (chicken in maize wine) and *mariscada* (seafood chowder).

$$ Kalpataru, Calle La Mascota 928 and Calle Maquilishuat, just below **Arbol de Dios**. Open until 2230, full restaurant service and lunch buffet, nice atmosphere. Best vegetarian place in town.

$$ KREEF, Plaza Kreef, 87 Av Sur and Av los Almendros Block G, Zona 11, Urb Maquilishuat T2264-7094, www.kreef.com. Restaurant and deli, specialities meat and juicy chicken filets, imported cheese, beer and wine. Live music weekends.

$$ Restaurante Sol y Luna, Blv Universitario, in front of **Cines Reforma**, T2225-6637. Mon-Fri 0830-1730, Sat until 1600. Delicious vegetarian food.

$$ Zócalo Escalón, 71 Av Norte, T2257-6851, next to Galerías mall. Excellent Mexican food in small, casual place, with outdoor tables; other branches around city, including Zona Rosa, San Benito and Santa Elena.

$$-$ Mercadito Merliot, Antiguo Cuscatlán. Famous food market with fresh seafood dishes (among others).

$ The Brother, Calle San Antonio Abad. Meats grilled on outdoor BBQ, large dishes and low prices.

$ Uncle Yang, Paseo General Escalón, T2264-7118. Taiwanese rice and noodle dishes, huge portions (*grande* is big enough for 2); try the Taiwanese iced tea with little tapioca dumplings sucked up through a wide straw. Clean, tasty and great value.

Cafés, delis and juice stalls

There are numerous cafeterías serving cheap traditional meals such as *tamales*, *pupusas*,

frijoles, rice with vegetables, etc. Often these places can be found around the major hotels.

Café de Don Pedro, Roosevelt y Alameda, next to Esso filling station. Good range of food, mariachi groups, open all night, another branch in Chiltiuapan, near Plaza Merliot Mall, also 24 hrs.

Oh-la-la, 1 Calle Ote and 69 Av Norte 168, just around the corner of Galerías mall, T2223-0161. Fine pastries.

Shakes, 3 Calle Pte 5254, Lomas Verdes, Col Escalón, T2263-4533. Juice bar and delicious fresh cakes. Recommended.

Shaw's, Paseo Escalón, 1 block west of Plaza Beethoven, Zona Rosa and at Metrocentro. Pricey but good coffee and chocolates, also sell US magazines, a few English-language books and greetings cards.

Entertainment

San Salvador *p16, maps p18 and p20*
Bars and clubs
Check for gigs in *La Prensa Gráfica* and *El Diario de Hoy*. All leading hotels have their own nightclub. All discos have ladies' night on Wed and Thu when women enter free and get a discount on drinks; go in a group.
Zona Rosa, **Col San Benito**, has many bars/discos/open-air cafés in a 5-block area, well-lit, crowded Fri-Sat night (disco cover charge is US$10), take bus No 30 B from near Esso/Texaco/Mundo Feliz on Blv de los Héroes before 2000, taxi thereafter. Just beyond Zona Rosa, the shopping malls of **Multiplaza** and **La Gran Vía** are the favourite places for going out; both have strips of night clubs, coffee shops and bars where young people gather at the weekends. Among the most popular discos in Multiplaza are **Envy** and **Stanza** and the bar **La Cueva**.
Café La T, run by German Anne, opposite Centro Comercial San Luis also has a fairtrade gift shop.
El Arpa Irlandés Av A 137 Col San José, run by Gerry from Ireland.

La Luna, Calle Berlín 228, off Blv de los Héroes, Urbanización Buenos Aires 3, T2260-2921, www.lalunacasayarte.com. Open Wed-Sun. Great food and atmosphere, live music some nights, decor and furniture designed by local artists. Popular and fashionable place to hang out. Reasonably priced drinks and snacks; take taxi late at night.

Photo Café, Col El Roble, Pje 2 21, T2100-2469, near National University, is an artsy place run by photojournalists.

Cinema

A few older-style cinemas in the centre are being overshadowed by the multiplexes along the Blv de los Héroes; most screenings are in English with Spanish subtitles. Look in local press for listings. Arthouse films are shown at **La Luna** and **Café La T** for free. See schedules for events. **Alliance Française** arranges film seasons, T2223-8084.

Music, dance and theatre

Ballet and theatre at the **Teatro Nacional de Bellas Artes**, and music or plays at the **Teatro Cámera**.

Spectator sports

Check *La Prensa Gráfica* and *El Diario de Hoy*.
Baseball On the field opposite Mercado Nacional de Artesanías, Tue-Fri 1700, Cuban and US coaches, local teams, entrance US$1.25.
Boat racing Club Náutico, at the Estero de Jaltepeque, is famous for its boat races across the mud flats at low tide.
Football Sun and Thu at the Cuscatlán and/or Flor Blanca stadiums.
Motor racing At the El Jabalí autodrome on lava fields near Quetzaltepeque.

✱ Festivals and events

San Salvador *p16, maps p18 and p20*
Mar/Apr Holy Week.
Jul/Aug Celebrations of **El Salvador del Mundo** are held the fortnight preceding 6 Aug. As a climax, colourful floats wend their way up the Campo de Marte (the park encompasssing Parque Infantil and Palacio de Deportes; 9 Calle Pte and Av España). On 5 Aug, an ancient image of the Saviour is borne before the large procession, before church services the next day, celebrating the **Feast of the Transfiguration**.
12 Dec Día del Indígena; there are colourful processions honouring the **Virgen de Guadalupe** (take bus No 101 to the Basílica de Guadalupe, on the Carretera a Santa Tecla).

✪ Shopping

San Salvador *p16, maps p18 and p20*
Visa and MasterCard are accepted in most establishments.

Bookshops

Magazines and newspapers in English can be bought at leading hotels and many shops sell US magazines. **Cervantes**, 9 Av Sur 114 in the Centre and Edif El Paseo 3, Paseo Escalón; **Clásicos Roxsil**, 6 Av Sur 1-6, Santa Tecla, T2228-1212; **Editorial Piedra Santa**, Av Olímpica 3428, Av 65-67 Sur, T2223-5502; **Etc Ediciones** in Centro Comercial Basilea, San Benito. Some English books at Librería Cultural Salvadoreña in Metrosur.
Olivos, also café and restaurant, just below Hotel Princess, Zona Rosa, T2245-4221, www.olivoscafe.com. Has a wide selection of books, specializing in alternative medicine and health.

Crafts

You can buy fairtrade arts and crafts at **Café La T**, Calle San Antonio Abad, and **Nahanché**. Metrocentro, Centro Comercial Basilea and Multiplaza has a great selection of handicrafts from all over the country.
El Arbol de Dios, La Mascota y Av Masferrer, T2224-6200, see page 21.
Mercado Ex-Cuartel, 8 Av Norte, 1 Calle Ote. Crafts market, a few blocks east of the Teatro Nacional, rebuilt after a fire in 1995.

Mercado Nacional de Artesanías, opposite the Estado Mayor on the road to Santa Tecla (buses 101A, B or C, 42B, 79, 34, 30B), at prices similar to the Mercado Ex-Cuartel, open daily 0800-1800. A 1-stop craft shop with a good cross-section of items even if not that well presented. Some of the cheapest prices.

Markets and malls

Metrocentro, large shopping mall on the Blv de los Héroes, northwest of the city centre. Together with **Metrosur** this is the largest shopping mall in Central America. Another shopping centre, **Villas Españolas**, is on the Paseo Escalón, 1 block south of the Redondel Masferrer; it is more exclusive, with expensive boutiques. **Galerías Escalón**, Col Escalón, has department stores and cybercafés. **El Paseo**, is the newish mall in Escalón, located just at the corner of 79 Av The area west of Zona Rosa has 3 newer malls named **Multiplaza, Hiper Mall Cascadas** and **La Gran Vía**.

▲ Activities and tours

San Salvador *p16, maps p18 and p20*
Tour operators
Inter Tours, Balam Quitze mall in Paseo Escalon, T2263-6188, www.viajero.com.sv. One of the most recognized travel agencies in the capital. They have excellent service and can track down that special rate you need.
OTEC Turismo Joven, Centro Comercial El Partenope, local 2, Paseo Escalón, T2264-0200, www.otec.com.sv. Official ISIC office in El Salvador and STA Travel representative, offering travel assistance, reissue of lost tickets, date changes and rerouting. Special prices for student, teacher and youth with ISIC card.
Pullmantur, Av La Revolución, T2243-1300. Luxury bus service to Guatemala and excellent package tours to Antigua.
Salva Natura, 33 Av Sur 640, Col Flor Blanca, T2279-1515, www.salvanatura.org. For information about Parque Nacional El Imposible in the southwest, near Tacuba and Ataco.
Tour In El Salvador, T2207-4155, www.tour inelsalvador.com. Minibus tours around the country and to Guatemala and Honduras; experienced and very knowledgeable guide Jorge Martínez. Highly recommended.

Watersports

El Salvador Divers, Paseo Escalón 3 Calle Pte 5020, Col Escalón, T2264-0961, www.elsalvadordivers.com. Offer weekly excursions and classes. Located behind the Villavicencio Mall.
Ríos Aventuras, is part of **Tropic Tours**, Av Olímpica 3597, T2279-3235, www.rios aventuras.com.sv. Bilingual guides organize rafting trips to Río Paz on the Guatemalan border. Recommended.

◉ Transport

San Salvador *p16, maps p18 and p20*
Air
The international airport (**SAL**), T2339-9455, at Comalapa is 62 km southeast from San Salvador towards Costa del Sol beach. **Acacya** minibus to airport, from 3 Calle Pte y 19 Av Norte, T2271-4937, airport T2339-9182, at 0600, 0700, 1000, 1400 (be there 15 mins before), US$3 one-way (leaves from airport when full, on right as you go out). **Acacya**, T2271-4937, also has a taxi service, US$25, the same as other radio taxi companies; ordinary taxis charge US$20. Taxi to **La Libertad** beach US$30. To **Costa del Sol** US$50. There is a post office, a tourist office, 2 exchange desks (including Citi Bank) and duty-free shopping for both departures and arrivals.

The old airport is at Ilopango, 13 km east of the city and is primarily used by the air force and for some domestic flights.

Airline offices American Airlines, Alameda Roosevelt, Edificio Centro-americana, 3107, T2298-0777. **Copa Airlines**, T2209-2600, www.copaair.com. **Delta**, 81 Av Norte y Calle El Mirador,

Edif WTC, local 107, piso 4, Col Escalón T2275-9292, www.delta.com. **Grupo TACA**, Oficinas Centrales Santa Elena (behind American Embassy), T2267-8222, www.taca.com. **Mexicana**, Edif Mejicana de Aviación, 2 nivel, Km 4.5, Carretera Sta Tecla, T2252- 9999, www.mexicana.com. **United Airlines**, T2279-3900, www.united.com.

Bus
Local Most buses stop running at 2100. City buses charge US$0.20 and microbuses charges US$0.25 within the city – have the right change or a small bill to hand. Most run 0500-2000, after which use taxis.

Some useful routes: No 29 from Terminal de Oriente to Metrocentro via downtown; **No 30** Mercado Central to Metrocentro; **No 30B** from Mundo Feliz (100 m up from Esso station on Blv de los Héroes) to Escalón, 79 Av Norte, Zona Rosa (San Benito), Alameda Roosevelt and back to Metrocentro along 49 Av; **No 34** San Benito–Mercado de Artesanías–Terminal de Occidente–Mercado Central–Terminal Oriente; **No 52** 'Paseo' Parque Infantil–Metrocentro–Plaza Las Américas– Paseo Escalón–Plaza Masferrer; **No 52** 'Hotel' Parque Infantil–Metrocentro–Hotel Copa Airlines–Plaza Masferrer. Route **No 101** buses to/from Santa Tecla are blue and white for either class of service.

Long distance and international
Domestic services go from **Terminal de Occidente**, off Blv Venezuela, T2223-3784 (take city buses 4, 7C, 27, 44 or 34); **Terminal de Oriente**, end of Av Peralta in Centro Urbano Lourdes (take city buses No 29 from Metrocentro, 42 from Alameda, or No 4, from 7 Calle), T2281-3086, very crowded with buses and passengers, keep your eyes open for the bus you want; and **Terminal Sur**, San Marcos, Zona Franca, about 9 km from the city (take city bus No 26 from Universidad Nacional area or Av España downtown,

take taxi to city after 1830). Terminal de Sonsonate, located just outside city centre, by main road to Acajutla T2450-4625, Terminal de Santa Ana T2440-0938. Routes and fares are given under destinations. For La Libertad and beaches west to Playa El Zonte, plenty of buses go from opposite Iglesia Ceiba Guadalupe, short taxi ride from centre: Bus No 102 to La Libertad and Nos 107 or 192 to Playa El Zonte, approx 1 hr, US$1.

Heading south: Recognized international bus company **Ticabus** departs from Hotel San Carlos, Calle Concepción 121, T2222-4808, www.ticabus.com. Also with an office in Blv del Hipódromo, Zona Rosa, T2243-9764. To **Tapachula** 0600 and 1200 noon, 11 hrs, US$30. To **Guatemala**, 0600 and 1300, 5 hrs, US$15. To **Tegucigalpa**, 1200, 7 hrs, US$15. To **Managua**, 0500, 12 hrs, US$30. To **San José**, 33 hrs including overnight in Managua, US$50. To **Panama City**, depart 0500, arriving 1700 next day, US$75. They now have an executive coach service to **Nicaragua** for US$44, and **Costa Rica** US$58 (both depart 0300) and to **Panama** at 0500, US$93. **King Quality**, Puerto Bus Terminal, Alameda Juan Pablo II y 19 Av Norte, T2241-8704; in Zona Rosa T2271-1361, www.king-qualityca.com. You can walk there from city centre, but it's not advisable with luggage; take bus 101D from Metrocentro, or bus 29, 52 to 21 Av Norte, 2 blocks south of terminal (city buses don't permit heavy luggage). The terminal has a *casa de cambio* (good rates) and a restaurant. They have departures to Central America and Mexico. Departure times from Puerto Bus station (check office for times from Zona Rosa).

Service to Guatemala with domestic carriers include **Pezzarossi**, **Taca**, **Transesmer**, **Melva**, and **Vencedora**. All operate services to **Guatemala City** more or less hourly (5½ hrs, US$13). Departures between 0500 and 1600. **Confortlines** (sister company of **King**

Quality) has departures to Guatemala at 0800 and 1400 for US$30 – higher-class bus than the regular service but no meals. **Pullmantur**, T2243-1300, runs a 0700 service Mon-Sat, 0830 Sun, and a daily luxury 1500 service from Hotel Marriott Presidente in Zona Rosa for US$35, with a/c, film, drinks and meals.

Service to Mexico also from Terminal de Occidente, **El Cóndor** goes to **Talismán**, Mexico via Sonsonate, La Hachadura and Escuintla, US$12, 0330, 9½ hrs, also 0700-0800 to Guatemala City. **Transgalgos** has direct departures to Mexico from Puerto Bus.

Car
Car hire Local insurance (about US$10-15 per day plus a deductible US$1000 deposit) is mandatory and 13% IVA applies. **Avis**, 43 Av Sur 137, Col. Flor Blanca www.avis. com.sv, T2500-2847; **Budget**, Hotel Sheraton Presidente, Col San Benito T2283-2908 and Calle Mirador and 85 Av Norte 648, Col Escalón, T2264-3888, www.budget.com; **Hertz**, corner of 91 Av Nte and 9 Calle Pte, T2264-2818, www.hertz.com; **Sandoval & Co**, T2235-4405, sub-compact late-model cars from US$10 per day, English spoken; **Euro Rent-Cars**, 29 Calle Pte and 7 Av Norte 1622, T2235-5232, chamba_r@hotmail.com, cheap daily rates from US$10.

Car repairs Modern service centres of **Record** and **Impressa**, are found throughout the capital. Good source of spare parts found at **Super Repuestos**, T2221-4440.

Insurance **Asesuiza** is widely used for car insurance T2209-5025 as is **La Centroamericana**, T2298-6666.

Car papers Ministerio de Hacienda, T2226-1900, 'Tres Torres', turn left on Blv de los Héroes, 300 m past Texaco station.

Taxi
Plenty (all yellow), don't have meters, ask fare before getting in. Trips within San Salvador will have a mininum cost of US$4 and most trips will be between US$4 and US$7. Airport is approximately US$25. Few drivers speak English. They will charge more in the rain. More expensive radio taxis may be hired through **Acacya**, T2271-4937.

🄳 Directory

San Salvador p16, maps p18 and p20
Banks
Most banks open Mon-Fri 0900-1600, Sat 0900-1200. The banks have branches in all the shopping malls and in large hotels such as **Princess Hilton** and **Radisson**. ATMs only give US dollars. **Banco Agrícola Comercial de El Salvador**, Paseo Escalón 3635, T2279-1033, English spoken. **HSBC** give good rates for TCs and Visa card advances. Most banks give cash advance on your credit card if you bring your passport. In emergency, for Visa International or MasterCard, T2224-5100; Visa TCs can only be changed by Visa cardholders. Visa ATMs can be found at **Aval** card 24-hr machines, the majority at Esso and Shell service stations (eg Esso, Blv de los Héroes), but also at Metrocentro, 8th floor food court, and Centro de Servicio, Av Olímpica. See also Yellow Pages. **Western Union** for money transfers, c/o **HSCB** branches, T2225-2503 (48 other branches throughout the country, look out for the black and yellow sign), head office Alameda Roosevelt 2419 between 45 y 47 Av Sur, T2298-1888, Mon-Fri 0800-1700, Sat 0800-1200, take passport and photographic ID (30 mins if from USA/Canada, 2-3 hrs from Europe). **Banco de América Central** (Ex-Credomatic), next to Siman in Metrocentro and CC San Luis gives cash advances on credit cards.

Cultural centres
Alianza Francesa, 5 Av Norte 152, Col Escalón, T2260-5807 and newer location

in Col San Benito: Calle La Mascota 547, Pasaje 2, www.afelsalvador.com. **Union Church**, Calle 4 Final, Col La Mascota, T2263-8246, English-speaking interdominational international church, weekly church services and bible studies, volunteering opportunities. **Centro de Intercambio y Solidaridad (CIS)**, Blv Universitario 4, next to Cine Reforma, T2226-2623, www.cis-elsalvador.org, for language classes, FMLN (Frente Farabundo Martí para la Liberación Nacional) programmes and schools. **Instituto para el Rescate Ancestral Indígena Salvadoreño (RAIS)**, Av Santiago 20, Col San Mateo, has programmes for local aid to indigenous communities and the Nahual language and customs.

Embassies and consulates

Belize, Calle el Bosque Ote y Calle Lomas de Candelaria I, Block "P1", Col Jardines de la 1a Cima Etapa, T2248-1423. **Costa Rica**, Calle Cuscatlán 4415, between 81 and 83 Av Sur, Col Escalón, T2264-3863. **Canada**, Centro Financiero Gigante and Alameda Roosevelt y 63 Av Sur Lobby 2, local 6, T2279-4659. **France**, 1 Calle Pte 7380, Col Escalón, T2298-4260. **Germany**, 77 Av Norte y 7 Calle Pte 3972, T2263-2088. **Guatemala**, 15 Av Norte 135 between 1 Calle Pte and Calle Arce, T2271-2225. **Holland**, I Calle Pte 3796, T2298-2185. **Honduras**, 89 Av Norte 561, between 7 and 9 Calle Pte, Col Escalón, T2263-2808. **Israel**, Centro Financiero Gigante, Torre B, 11 piso, Alameda Roosevelt y 63 Av Sur, T2211-3434. **Italy**, La Reforma 158, Col San Benito, T2223-4806. **Mexico**, Pasaje 12 y Calle Circunvalación, San Benito, behind Hotel Presidente, T2248-9906. **Nicaragua**, Calle Mirador and 93 Av Norte 4814, Col Escalón, T2263-8849. **Norway**, Calle Cuscatlán 133 between 83 and 81 Av Sur, Col Escalón, T2263-8257. **Panama**, Av Buganvilia No21, Col San Francisco T2298-0773. **Spain**, Calles la Reforma 164, Col San Benito, T2257-5700. **Sweden**, Alameda Manuel E Araujo y 67 Av Sur 3515, T2281-7901. **Switzerland**, Pastelería Lucerna, 85 Av Sur y Paseo Escalón 4363, T2263-7485. **USA**, Blv Santa Elena, Antiguo Cuscatlán, T2278-4444, outside the city, reached by bus 101A.

Emergency

Fire service, T2555-7300. **Red Cross**, Av Henry Dunat y 17 Av Norte, T2224-5155, 24-hr. **Police**, T911, no coin needed from new coin phones. In San Salvador, metropolitan police deal with tourist complaints.

Immigration

Departamento de Inmigración, Centro de Gobierno, T2221-2111, Mon-Fri 0800-1600. Will consider extending tourist visas, but be prepared with photos and plenty of patience. **Migración y Extranjería**, Plaza Merliot and Hipermall Cascadas saves the trip to Centro de Gobierno and has quicker service.

Internet

Cafés (roughly US$1 per hr) are found throughout the city, especially at shopping malls.

Language schools

Centro de Intercambio y Solidaridad, Blv Universitario 4, T2226-2623, www.cisel salvador.org. Spanish school in the mornings 0800-1200, English school in the afternoons 1700-1900 (volunteer English teachers needed for 10-week sessions). **Cihuatan Spanish Language Institute** (Ximena's Guest House), Calle San Salvador 202, Col Centro América (near Hotel Real Intercontinental), T2260-2481, ximenas@ navegante.com.sv; US$8 per hr.

Libraries

The **UCA** library (Universidad Centro-americana), José S Cañas, Autopista Sur, is said to be the most complete collection. US information library at **American Chamber of Commerce**, 87 Av Norte 720, Apto A, Col Escalón, Apdo Postal (05) 9, Sr Carlos Chacón, speaks English, helpful. **Centro Cultural Salvadoreño**, Av Los Sisimiles, Metrocentro Norte, T2226-9103, 0800-1100, 1400-1700, English library, excellent. **Intercambios Culturales de El Salvador**, 67 Av Sur 228, Col Roma, T2245-1488, extensive Spanish and English reference library, local artistic exhibitions, computer school.

Medical services
Hospitals and clinics Hospital de la **Mujer**, between 81 and 83 Av Sur y Calle Juan José Cañas, Col Escalón (south of Paseo, bus 52 Paseo), T2263-5181. **Hospital Pro-Familia**, 25 Av Norte 483, 11 blocks east of Metrocentro, T2244-8000, clinics and 24-hr emergency, reasonable prices. **Hospital Rosales**, 25 Av Norte y 3 Calle Pte, T2231-9200, long waits. **Clínicas Médicas**, 25 Av Norte 640 (bus 3, 9, 44 centro from Universidad Nacional), T2225-5233. If you contract a serious stomach problem, the doctor will send you for tests, which will cost US$5-6. **Doctors** Dr Cesar Armando **Solano**, at Av Bernal 568, Col Yurimuri T2261-1657, excellent dentist and low prices. English spoken. **Medicentro La Esperanza**, 27 Av Norte is a good place to find doctors

in most specialist fields, afternoons mostly after 1500. **Dr Jorge Panameno**, T2225-9928, English-speaking, specialist in tropical diseases, makes house calls at night for about US$50.

Post
Central Post Office at the Centro de Gobierno with EMS, T2527-7600. Good service to Europe. Mon-Fri 0730-1700, Sat 0730-1200. **Lista de Correos**, Mon-Fri 0800-1200, 1430-1700, good service for mail collection. Branches throughout the city.

Telephone
Phone boxes throughout the city, card only, available at fast-food stores such as **Pollo Campero**; direct dialling to anywhere in the world, also collect calls. Telephone cards for sale in pharmacies and stores, denominations from US$1 upwards.

Work
UCA University Simeon Cañas, Blv Los Próceres San Salvador, T2210-6600, www.uca.edu.sv. An English-language programme always needing certified English teachers.

Western El Salvador

Compact and with good transport links, Western El Salvador combines the dramatic volcanic landscapes of Cerro Verde, Volcán Izalco and Lago de Coatepeque – essential for any visitor to the country – with the serene beauty and majesty of countless waterfalls and the colourful Ruta de las Flores around Sonsonate. Little indigenous villages and pre-Columbian ruins contrast with the vibrancy of Santa Ana, El Salvador's second largest city. Three routes lead to Guatemala, the northernmost passing close to the impressive cloud forests of Parque Nacional Montecristo on the border with Honduras.

Izalco to Sonsonate → *For listings, see pages 42-48.*

From the junction with the Pan-American Highway, just west of Colón, route CA 8 heads west, past Armenia, to the town of **Izalco** (population: 70,959) at the foot of Izalco volcano (8 km from Sonsonate, bus 53C). The town has evolved from the gradual merging of the *ladino* village of Dolores Izalco and the indigenous village of Asunción Izalco. In colonial times this was an important trading centre and experienced a communist rebellion in 1932. Today the town is experiencing a tourist revival with good colonial architecture, a prominent and active indigenous population, and rich heritage of religious imagery which blends indigenous and Roman Catholic beliefs, and produces regular processions and festivals. A week-long festival celebrating El Salvador del Mundo runs 8-15 August and there is also a local celebration from 24 November to 10 December. The Feast of John the Baptist runs from 17-24 June.

Note The town of Izalco and Izalco volcano are not directly connected by road. A paved road branches off the Pan-American Highway 14 km before the turning for Izalco town (about 22 km from Sonsonate) and goes up towards Cerro Verde, Volcán Izalco and Lago de Coatepeque (see page 36).

Sonsonate and around → *For listings, see pages 42-48. Altitude: 225 m. Population: 71,541.*

Sonsonate, 64 km from the capital, is the country's chief cattle-raising region. It also produces sugar, tobacco, rice, tropical fruits, hides and balsam. The city was founded in 1552 and is hot, dirty and crowded, but worth checking to see the colonial architecture in the city centre. The beautiful **El Pilar** church (1723) is strongly reminiscent of the church of El Pilar in San Vicente. The **cathedral** has many cupolas (the largest covered with white porcelain) and was badly damaged in the 2001 earthquake but is now fully restored. The old church of **San Antonio del Monte** (completed 1861), 1 km from the city, draws pilgrims from afar (fiesta 22-26 August). There is a small **railway museum**, look for the locomotive at the entrance to the city on the highway from San Salvador (Km 65). An important market is held each Sunday. The market outside the church is quite well organized. In the northern outskirts of the city there is a waterfall on the Río Sensunapán. Legend has it that an indigenous princess drowned there, and on the anniversary of her death a gold casket appears below the falls. The main annual event is **Feria de la Candelaria** in February. Easter Week processions are celebrated with particular fervour and are probably the most impressive in the whole country. On Easter Thursday and Holy Friday the streets are filled with thousands of members of the *cofradías* (brotherhoods).

Around Sonsonate

Route CA 8, northwest to Ahuachapán (see page 39), has spectacular scenery along the **Ruta de las Flores**, with frequent buses from Sonsonate (bus 249 and 285, two hours) covering the 40-km paved route. The road goes just outside the indigenous village of **Nahuizalco** (population: 49,081). Some of the older women here still wear the *refajo* (a doubled length of cloth made of tie-dyed threads worn over a wrap-round skirt), and various crafts are still made, including wood and rattan furniture. Although use of the indigenous language is dying out, you do still encounter people who speak Náhuatl. The night market, unique in El Salvador, opens at dusk and has traditional local food on sale. There's a religious festival 19-25 June, with music, **Danza de los Historiantes** and art exhibitions; also 24-25 December, with music and **Danza de los Pastores**. Take bus 53 D from Sonsonate.

Salcoatitán and Juayúa

A little further up the mountainside at Km 82 is **Salcoatitán** (population: 5484) at 1045 m above sea level, a colonial village with a beautiful park in front of the colonial church. This cosy village used to be only a drive-through on the way to Juayúa or Apaneca but has experienced a tourist revival lately with several new restaurants, art galleries and artisans shops. **Los Patios restaurant** (same owners Las Cabañas de Apaneca) just opened a restaurant and art gallery here.

Further along, the road branches off to Juayúa 2 km further north and the same bus from Sonsonate takes a detour into the village and back. **Juayúa** is the largest city on the Ruta de Las Flores – the name means 'River of Purple Orchids' in the local Náhuatl dialect – and sits nestled in a valley dominated by volcanoes. It's a peaceful spot where you can watch people at work and kids playing in the semi-cobbled street. The surrounding region is blanketed in coffee groves; the bean was introduced to the area in 1838 and today the town produces about 10% of the coffee exported from El Salvador. Its church houses an image of the **Cristo Negro** (Black Christ) carved by Quirio Cataño at the end of the 16th century. **Tourist information** is available from Jaime Salgado, at **Juayutur** ① *T2469-2310, juayutur@navegante.com.sv*. He can provide good information about the activities available in the region, which include rappelling waterfalls, the hike of the seven waterfalls and the mountain lagoon with wild horses. Guides are trained local youngsters. Also check out the **Casa de la Cultura**, on the corner next to the park for information on Juayúa. Gaby and Julio Vega, the owners of **Akwaterra Tours** ① *www.akwaterra.com*, run a mountain cabin at Finca Portezuelo named **La Escondida**; also a camping site with ready made-up tents on decks under covers. They're fluent in English and offer a wide range of activites at **Portezuelo**

Adventure Park such as hiking, mountain biking, horseback riding, zip-wire circuit, ATVs and paragliding.

There are a number of excursions you can do in the area to see wildlife, including river otters, toucans, butterflies and many other animals. In the dry season **Laguna de las Ranas** (Laguna Seca) dries up, attracting numerous reptiles as it shrinks. There are also trips to the 30-m-high waterfall at **Salto el Talquezal**, the 50-m-high **Salto de la Lagunilla Azul** and several other waterfalls in the region (seven in one day if you take a tour), with swimming and picnics on the way (see below). Every weekend Juayúa celebrates the Feria Gastronómica, an opportunity to try a variety of traditional dishes, often accompanied by local events, music and shows.

The **Feria Gastrónomica Internacional** is in January and celebrates with dishes from all over the world; other festivals include **Día de los Canchules** (31 October), when people ask for candies and **Día de las Mercedes** (17 September), when the houses are decorated with branches and candles leading up to the procession of the Virgen de la Merced. Another local attraction is the **Museo del Café**, of the coffee cooperative **La Majada** ① *T2467-9008 ext 1451, www.cafemajadaoro.com.sv*, located in **San José La Majada**, just outside Juayua on the road to Los Naranjos. Tours include information on coffee processing and a trip to the processing plant. A coffee shop offers local brews and iced coffee.

Los Naranjos and around

Moving northeast of Juayúa, swirling up a scenic mountain road connecting Juayúa with Santa Ana you arrive at Los Naranjos, a small traditional coffee village located at the mountain pass between Santa Ana and the Pilón volcanoes. The lines of wind-breaking trees preventing damage to coffee trees are particularly beautiful, while the high altitude makes the climate cool with the scent of cypress forests. A series of restaurants and small cabins for lodging has popped up in recent years and is an excellent option for cool climate and countryside relaxation.

At Km 82 on the Carretera Salcoatitán to Juayúa is **Parque y Restaurante La Colina** ① *T2452-2916, www.lacolinajuayua.com*, with hammocks, arts and crafts, and horse riding available. **Apaneca** is a short distance uphill from Sonsonate, see page 33.

Several **waterfalls** and other sites of natural beauty can be found in the Sonsonate district. To the west, near the village of **Santo Domingo de Guzmán** (bus 246 from Sonsonate), are the falls of **El Escuco** (2 km north), **Tepechapa** (1.5 km further) and **La Quebrada** (further still up the Río Tepechapa), all within walking distance of both Santo Domingo and each other. Walk through the town, then follow the river, there are several spots to swim. Santo Domingo de Guzmán is also known for its *alfarería* (pottery) of *comales*, clay plates used to create tortillas and *pupusas* over the open fire, and its many Náhuatl-speaking habitants. There's a festival in Santo Domingo, 24-25 December. A short distance north is **San Pedro Puxtla** (bus 246), with a modern church built on the remains of an 18th-century edifice. From here you can visit the **Tequendama Falls** on the Río Sihuapán. Bus 219 goes east to **Cuisnahuat** (18th-century baroque church), where the Fiesta de San Judas takes place 23-29 November. From there it is 2 km south to the Río Apancoyo, or 4 km north to **Peñón El Escalón** (covered in balsam trees) and **El Istucal Cave**, at the foot of the Escalón hill, where indigenous rites are celebrated in November.

Santa Tecla to Santa Ana → *For listings, see pages 42-48.*

The new Pan-American Highway parallels the old one, continuing northwest to the border with Guatemala at San Cristóbal. Santa Ana, acting as a transport hub, has routes out to Ahuachapán to the west and the border at Las Chinamas, as well as north to Metapán and beyond to the border crossing of Anguiatú.

Fifteen kilometres from Santa Tecla, 7 km beyond the junction with the Sonsonate road, there is a junction to the right. This road forks immediately, right to **Quezaltepeque**, left (at Joya de Cerén café) to **San Juan Opico**. After a few kilometres on the San Juan road, you cross the railway by the Kimberley-Clark factory.

Joya de Cerén
ⓘ *US$3, parking US$1, T2401-5782, www.fundar.org.sv/joyadeceren.*
After the girder bridge crossing the Río Sucio there is a grain store beside which is Joya de Cerén (32 km from the capital). This is a major archaeological site and on the World Heritage List of UNESCO (the only one in El Salvador), not for spectacular temples, but because this is the only known site where ordinary Maya houses have been preserved having been buried by the ash from the nearby Laguna Caldera volcano in about AD 600. Buildings and construction methods can be clearly seen; a painted book and household objects have been found. All the structures are covered with protective roofing. The site has a small but good museum, café, toilets and car park. Official tours are in Spanish but English-language tours are available upon request. ▶▶ *See Transport, page 47.*

San Andrés
ⓘ *Tue-Sun 0900-1600, US$3, popular for weekend picnics, otherwise it's quiet. Has a café. Take bus No 201 from Terminal de Occidente, US$1.50 (same bus from Santa Ana) T2319-3220, www.fundar.org.sv/sanandres.*
Back on the main road, heading west is the excavated archaeological site of San Andrés, halfway between Santa Tecla and Coatepeque on the estate of the same name (its full name is **La Campana de San Andrés**). It is located at Km 32.5 on the Pan-American Highway, just after the Hilasal towel factory. A **museum** at the site displays some of the ceramics found (others can be seen at the Museo Nacional de Antropología David J Guzmán – MUNA – in San Salvador, see page 21). The museum also features a special indigo section with information about this natural dye. El Salvador was the number one producer of indigo in the world during the colonial era. A large indigo *obraje* (processing basin) – probably the largest found in Latin America – was found at San Andrés during an archaeological excavation and has been preserved. There are good views of the nearby hills.

Lago de Coatepeque
At El Congo, 13 km before Santa Ana, a branch road leads south to the northern shore of the beautiful Lago de Coatepeque, a favourite weekend resort, with good sailing, watersports and fishing, near the foot of Santa Ana Volcano. Many weekend homes line the north and east shores, making access to the water difficult, but there are public *balnearios*. The lakeside hotels are a good option for having a meal and use their infrastructure for the day. You can also get boat rides on the lake through the hotels or by

Climbing Izalco

Izalco, as can be seen from the lack of vegetation, is a geologically young volcano. Historical records show that activity began in the 17th century as a sulphurous smoke vent but, in February 1770, violent eruptions formed a cone that was more or less in constant activity until 1957. There was a small eruption in 1966 through a blowhole on the southeast slope testified by two 1000-m lava flows. Since that time, it has been quiescent.

A path leads off the road (signposted) just below the car park on Cerro Verde. In 20-30 minutes, descend to the saddle between Cerro Verde and Izalco, then it's one to 1½ hours up (steep but manageable). The contrast between the green forest of Cerro Verde and the coal-black lava around Izalco is impressive. The climb is three hours from base. Beware of falling rocks when climbing. There's a spectacular view from the top so try to ensure that low cloud is not expected before planning to go. For a quick descent, find a rivulet of soft volcanic sand and half-slide, half-walk down in 15 minutes, then it's about one hour back up the saddle. This 'cinder running' requires care, strong shoes and consideration for those below.

If you wish to climb the volcano you need to take the first bus to Cerro Verde, as the park rangers wait for the passengers from this bus before they start the guided climb to the volcano at 1100.

---

independent fishermen. There are *aguas termales* (hot springs) on the opposite side of the lake. A ride is between US$15 and US$45. There are two islands in the lake – **Anteojos** which is close to the hotels, and **Teopán** on the far side. The local Fiesta del Santo Niño de Atocha runs from 25-29 June.

Cerro Verde, Volcán Izalco and Volcán Santa Ana

ⓘ *Park entrance US$1, passport or photocopy required, car park US$0.70. Guided tour to the summit of Izalco or Santa Ana is included, leaving from the entrance daily 1100. The guided tour through the nature trail around the Cerro Verde Summit is US$0.25 per person and is led by local trained guides. The Turicentro Cerro Verde (the summit of Cerro Verde with its trails, the parking lot and departure point for the hikes to the volcano) is run by the Ministry of Tourism, for information T2222-8000, www.elsalvador.travel. The whole area covering the volcanoes Santa Ana, Cerro Verde and Izalco and surrounding area are part of the Parque Nacional de los Volcanes, which is administrated by Salvanatura, T2279-1515, www.salvanatura.org.*
In October 2005, Santa Ana volcano erupted for the first time in more than 100 years. The area was closed for a period, but it has now reopened.

From El Congo another road runs south, around the east shore of Lago Coatepeque. This road is locally known as Carretera Panorámica, due to the fantastic view of Coatepeque on one side and the mountains and valleys beyond the ridge. After reaching the summit, the paved road branches right, climbing above the south end of the lake to **Parque Nacional Cerro Verde** (2030 m) with its fine and surprising views of the Izalco volcano (1910 m), and Santa Ana volcano (2381 m), the highest volcano in the country. The road up to Cerro Verde is lined with beautiful flowers and halfway up there is a mirador with a great view of Lago Coatepeque. Cerro Verde is probably one of the most beautiful places in El Salvador due to the special flora and fauna, breathtaking views and fine volcano trekking.

A 30-minute walk along a nature trail leads you around the crater ridge, to a series of miradors with views of Lago Coatepeque and Santa Ana volcano. For the best view of Izalco, go in the morning, although the afternoon clouds around the cone can be enchanting. *▶▶ For information on climbing Volcán Izalco, see box, page 37.*

The old hotel and its volcano-view terrace was destroyed in the 2001 earthquake but you can still go there for an amazing view over Izalco volcanic crater. There are now a couple of cabins available for US$35-55. For information call the **Turicentro** ① T7949-2751. To access Cerro Verde, take bus No 208 from Santa Ana at 0800, passing El Congo at 0815 am to catch the 1100 departure. If you come from Sonsonate side, take the No 209 bus from Sonsonate to Cerro Verde.

Santa Ana and around → *For listings, see pages 42-48. Altitude: 776 m. Population: 245,421.*

Santa Ana, 55 km from San Salvador and capital of its department, is the second largest city in the country. The basin of the Santa Ana volcano is exceptionally fertile, producing large amounts of coffee, with sugar cane coming a close second. The city, named Santa Ana La Grande by Fray Bernardino Villapando in 1567, is the business centre of western El Salvador. There are some fine buildings: the neo-Gothic **cathedral**, and several other churches, especially **El Calvario**, in neoclassical style. Of special interest is the classical **Teatro de Santa Ana** ① *on the north side of the plaza, a guide (small charge) will show you round on weekdays, refer to the local press for performances*, originally completed in 1910, now in the latter stages of interior restoration and one of the finest theatres in Central America. The Fiestas Julias take place from 1-26 July.

Chalchuapa → *Altitude: 640 m. Population: 96,727.*

About 16 km west of Santa Ana, on the road to Ahuachapán, lies Chalchuapa. President Barrios of Guatemala was killed in battle here in 1885, while trying to reunite Central America by force. There are some good colonial-style domestic buildings. The church of Santiago Apóstol is particularly striking; almost the only one in El Salvador which shows strong indigenous influences (restored 1997-1998). Fiestas are on 18-21 July, Santiago Apóstol, and 12-16 August, San Roque. **Tazumal** ruins next to the cemetery in Chalchuapa, are the tallest and probably the most impressive in El Salvador. Built about AD 980 by the Pipil, with its 14-step pyramid. In 2004 the ruins suffered a partial collapse of the main pyramid due to the filtration of water which led to extensive excavations and application of new preservation techniques (getting rid of the old concrete) and many new discoveries were made. The excavations concluded in 2006. The site has been occupied since 5000 BC and in the **Museo Stanley H Boggs** ① *Tue-Sun 0900-1600, T2408-4295*, you find artefacts found in Tazumal since the first excavations in the 1950s.

Casa Blanca Archaeological Site ① *Km 78 Pan-American Hwy, T2408-4641, Tue-Sun 0900-1600, US$1*, just outside Chalchuapa, has several pyramids, ongoing excavations, and a museum that provides an insight into the archaeology of the area and information on indigo (*añil*) production. If you want to participate in the indigo workshop the cost is US$3. It's very interesting, educational and you can keep the products produced. Recommended.

Atiquizaya

The road continues 12 km west to Atiquizaya, a small, quiet town with one *hospedaje*, several good *pupuserías* (1600-2100) and **Restaurante Atiquizaya**, which can be found at the intersection with the main highway to Ahuachapán. At **Cataratas del Río Malacachupán** there is a beautiful 50-m-high waterfall cascading into a lagoon; it's a 1-km hike to get there. Nearby is **Volcán Chingo** on the Guatemalan border. Another attraction is **Aguas Calientes**, a hot spring that runs into the river and is excellent for a relaxing bath and for enjoying nature. It's a short ride from Atiquizaya, but bring a local guide.

Ahuachapán → *Altitude: 785 m. Population: 110,511.*

A quiet town with low and simple houses, 35 km from Santa Ana. Coffee is the main product. The main local attraction is the geothermal field of **Los Ausoles**, 3 km road from Ahuachapan and marked on the road out of town to Apaneca as 'Planta Geotérmica'. You can't go into the plant, but when you arrive take the road to the right where, just a little way up the hill on the left, you come to a little house, geysers of boiling mud with plumes of steam and strong whiffs of sulphur. The *ausoles* are used for generating 30% of the country's electricity. For a small tip the house owner will take you into his back garden to see the fumaroles and boiling pools. If you want a more

Santa Ana

To Metapán

Sleeping
Casa Frolaz 5
El Faro 1
La Libertad 3
La Posada del Rey 2
Sahara 4

Eating
Expresión 1
Los Horcones 3
Lover's Steak House 2

professional tour, with an explanation on the thermal activity including a trip through the geothermal plant, contact **Tours Universales** in the city, see page 47.

Taking the northern road from Ahuachapán, 9 km west of town near the village of **Los Toles** are the **Tehuasilla Falls**, where the Río El Molino falls 60 m (bus No 293 from Ahuachapán to Los Toles, then walk 1 km). The road continues northwest through the treeless **Llano del Espino**, with its small lake, and across the Río Paz into Guatemala.

Tacuba → *Population: 29,585.*

Tacuba is an indigenous town, around 850 m above sea level, and 15 km west of Ahuachapán. Tacuba means 'the village of the football game', probably relating to the *juego de pelota* of the Maya, and the existence of many pre-Columbian mounds in the surrounding area suggest the region was heavily populated in the past. At the entrance to the town are the largest colonial church ruins in El Salvador, torn down by the earthquake of Santa Marta, the same tremors that ruined large parts of Antigua, Guatemala, in 1773. You can also visit the Casa de la Cultura office, **Concultura** ⓘ *3 km on main st north, daily 0900-1230, 1330-1600*, to see an interesting display of photos. The town is near the northern entrance of Parque Nacional El Imposible (see page 69), which is accessed by hiking or 4WD in the dry season.

The surrounding area offers a wide range of opportunities including waterfalls, pristine rivers, mountain hikes and panoramic views. **Ceiba de los Pericos**, 15 minutes out of Tacuba by car, a 600-year-old ceiba tree where thousands of parrots flock together at dusk to sleep in its branches, ending the day with a deafening noise before resting for the night. In Tacuba centre the **Ceiba de las Garzas** is the rendezvous of hundreds of *garzas* (herons).

Local tour company **El Imposible Tours**, led by Tacuba native Manolo González, provide tours of the Tacuba area and to Parque Nacional El Imposible (see page 69). The dirt road leading from Tacuba to the cordillera, is steep and spectacular and provides impressive views; it is recommended although a 4WD is required.

Apaneca → *Altitude: 1450 m. Population: 8383.*

Between Ahuachapán and Sonsonate is Apaneca (91 km from San Salvador, 29 km from Las Chinamas on the border) an extremely peaceful town (and the highest town in the country), with small cobbled streets, marking the summit of the **Ruta de las Flores**. Founded by Pedro de Alvarado in 1543, Apaneca is known for its cool climate and winds – *apaneca* means 'rivers of wind' in Náhuatl. The town has a colonial centre, a traditional *parque* and a municipal market selling fruit, flowers and handicrafts. One of the oldest parochial churches in the country used to corner the central park but was demolished after damage caused by the 2001 earthquake. It has been partially reconstructed, with a modern twist. The artisans market is a great place to see the local arts and crafts. Other local industries include coffee, flowers for export and furniture. Have a look at the topiary creations outside the police station. Check out the **Casa de la Cultura** in the centre of town. There are two small lakes nearby to the north, **Laguna Verde** and **Laguna Las Ninfas**, whose crater-like walls are clothed in tropical forest and cypress trees. It is possible to swim in the former, but the latter is too shallow and reedy. According to local legend, a swim is meant to be very beneficial to your health and the lakes are very popular with tourists. This is the Cordillera de Apaneca, part of the narrow highland belt running southeast of Ahuachapán.

South of Apaneca is the **Cascada del Río Cauta**. To get there, take bus No 216 from Ahuachapán towards Jujutla, alight 3 km after the turn-off to Apaneca, then walk 300 m along the trail to the waterfall.

Santa Leticia archaeological site ⓘ *US$2; 2-hr coffee tour US$20; both combined US$35, www.coffee.com.sv,* is believed to be 2600 years old and was rediscovered in 1968 by the farm owner. Three huge monuments are buried among the coffee groves and you feel like a first-time discoverer as you travel the winding route to get there. There are three stone spheres with human characteristics weighing between 6000 and 11,000 kg. To get there, take bus No 249 from Juayúa (10 minutes).

Ataco

Concepción de Ataco, to give the town its full name, located just below Apaneca, is now a favourite on the Ruta de Las Flores. The village has undergone a complete renovation, and now boasts cobbled streets, old-fashioned benches and street lights, and a popular weekend festival with food, flowers, and arts and crafts. Some excellent coffee shops and restaurants, offering cuisine from Mexico to France, continue to open up, mainly for weekends only, making Ataco one of the most visited villages in the area, and well worth a weekend trip.

Look for the *marimba* and the traditional dances in the main square and drop by **Diconte & Axul**, an artsy café that offers anything from delicious home-made pies to original arts and crafts that are giving La Palma art a run for their money. The **House of Coffee** has an espresso machine and serves the excellent world-class coffee grown in Ataco at their own *finca* for five generations.

North of Santa Ana

Texistepeque, 17 km north of Santa Ana on the road to Metapán, has an 18th-century baroque church, with fiestas on 23-27 December and 15 January. The town was one of the main areas for indigo production, and colonial processing plants known as *obrajes* exist all around the area. Visit the indigo workshop and museum of **Licenciado Marroquín** just out of town.

Metapán is about 10 km northeast of Lago de Güija and 32 km north of Santa Ana. Its colonial baroque **Catedral de San Pedro**, completed by 1743, is one of the very few to have survived in El Salvador. The altarpieces have some very good silver work, and the façade is splendid. The Fiesta de San Pedro Apóstol runs from 25-29 June. There are lots of easy walks with good views towards **Lago de Metapán** and, further on, **Lago de Güija**. If planning to walk in the hills near Metapán, seek local advice and do not walk alone. **Parque Acuático Apuzunga** ⓘ *20 mins' drive from Metapán towards Santa Ana, T2483-8952, www.apuzunga.com,* is an adventure park by the Río Guajoyo, with fun pools, slides, zip-wires and a range of activities, including whitewater rafting and kayaking. There's a restaurant overlooking the river offering great views of the rafts shooting the rapids and the zip-wire over the water.

Reserva Nacional y Natural Montecristo

① 20 km from Metapán to the park. Park employees (guardabosques) escort visitors and a permit is obtained (via fax or email) through MARN (Ministry of Environment) in San Salvador, T2267-6259 (with Patrimonio Natural and ask for Solicitud de Ingreso a Parque Nacional Montecristo). You need to fill out a form and pay US$6 per person. A 4WD is necessary in the wet season (mid-May to mid-Oct). To hire a 4WD and driver, contact Sr Francisco Xavier Monterosa, Calle 15 de Septiembre Casa 40, T2402-2805/T7350-1111 (mob). The trails to the summit take 4 hrs. Camping is permitted, with 3 campsites inside the park, spacious and clean, under the pine trees, with toilets, barbecue grills and picnic benches and tables. An overnight stay is needed if you want to reach the summit – worthwhile to fully appreciate the dramatic changes in vegetation as you climb from 800-2400 m above sea level.

A mountain track from Metapán gives access to El Salvador's last remaining cloud forest, where there is an abundance of protected wildlife. It now forms part of El Trifinio, or the International Biosphere 'La Fraternidad', administered jointly by Guatemala, Honduras and El Salvador. The summit of **Cerro Montecristo** (2418 m), is the point where the three borders meet, At the Casco Colonial, former finca, is a visitor centre, with small museum and wildlife exhibits. Nearby is an **orchid garden** with over 100 species (the best time to see them in flower is early spring), an orchard and a camping ground in the forest. The views are stunning, as is the change seen in flora and fauna with the altitude. This highest elevated part is closed for visitors during the mating and reproduction season of the animals (31 May to 31 October).

Western El Salvador listings

For Sleeping and Eating price codes and other relevant information, see page 10.

⊙ Sleeping

Izalco *p33*
$$ La Casona de Los Vega, 2a Av Norte 24, in the center of Izalco. T2453-5951, www.lacasonadelosvega.com.sv. Colonial home converted into comfortable hotel and restaurant with good views.
$ El Chele, Final Av Roberto Carillas, Calle La Violeta, Caserío Texcalito, T2453-6740. Ricardo Salazar, T7798-8079, www.izalcoel chelerestaurant.com, some 800 m north of Izalco at a *finca* surrounded by forest. Great view of Volcán Izalco. Escorted hikes and horse rides available to Cerro Verde and its surrounding slopes and Izalco with visits to 2 pre-Columbian ruins nearby. Free transport available, call to arrange. English spoken.

Sonsonate *p33*
$$ Agape, Km 63 on outskirts of town, take old road through Sonsonate, the hotel is on the exit street to San Salvador, just before the main roundabout on the right side, T2451-2667, www.hotelagape.com.sv. Converted convent, suites and rooms, a/c or fan, safe parking, fine restaurant, gardens, cable TV, pool and laundry service. Recommended.

Salcoatitán and Juayúa *p34*
$$-$ La Escondida, 6 km north of Juayúa at Finca El Portezuelo, T7888-4552, www.akwa terra.com. B&B in an exceptionally beautiful location, in a coffee plantation cradled between Laguna Verde and forest-clad mountains, with a view over to Ahuachapán to the north. Cosily furnished rooms, with fireplace, DVD, equipped kitchen. Contact Julio and Gaby (English spoken). They also

offer coffee decks – a tent protected by a roofed wooden structure – and camping.

$ Anahuac, 1 Calle Pte and 5 Av Norte, Juayúa, T2469-2401, www.hotelanahuac. com. Dormitories and private rooms for backpackers and tours, with garden, hammocks, book exchange. Very friendly owner Cesar also runs nearby **Café Cadejo** (live music at weekends); extremely popular and highly recommended.

$ Doña Mercedes, 29 Av Sur, 6 Calle Oriente 3-6, Juayúa, 1 block south of **Farmacia Don Bosco**, T2452-2287. Discounts for longer stays. Recommended.

$ El Mirador, a block from the park, Juayúa, T2452-2432, www.elmiradorjuayua.com. A 3-storey building with restaurant on top. Best option for low rates and central location.

$ Hostal Casa Mazeta, 4 blocks from main square opposite church, Juayúa, T2406-3403. Great backpackers' hostel in former family home, cosy rooms, dorm and covered hammock space, with garden, kitchen, Wi-Fi and lounge area with DVD library. French owner, also speaks English, German and Spanish. Tours, parking space and laundry. Recommended.

$ Hotel Juayúa, Urb Esmeralda, Final 6a Av Norte, Juayúa, T2469-2109, www.hoteljuayua.com. Newest hotel in town, with great views.

Los Naranjos and around *p35*
$$ Hotel and Restaurant Los Trozos, located on the road down to Sonsonate. T2415-9879, www.lostrozos.com.

Lago de Coatepeque *p36*
$$ Torremolinos, on pier out above the lagoon, T2441-6037, www.torremolinos lagocoatepeque.com. Pool, good rooms (all with hot showers), restaurant and bar, boating trips, popular at weekends with music, lively. Discounts for longer stays.

$ Amacuilco, 300 m from **Telecom**, T7822-4061.Very helpful manager called Sandra. 6 rooms undergoing renovation at time of writing but still open, with basic but clean and airy rooms, some with lake view, and hammocks. Discounts for longer stays, *marimba* classes, Spanish and Náhuatl lessons, and an art gallery. All meals available, pool, great view with jetty over the lake, secure, boat excursions on lake, tours arranged from US$30-40 per day, kayaks and bikes for rent. Recommended.

Santa Ana *p38, map p39*
Many hotels close their doors from 2000, so arrive early if you can.

$$ Sahara, 3 Calle Pte y 10 Av Sur, T2447-8865, www.hotelsahara.com.sv. Good service, but a little overpriced.

$ Casa Frolaz, 29 Calle Pte 42-B between 8 and 10 Av Sur T2440-5302, www.casafrolaz. com. Beautiful and clean hostel with art, paintings, history books and a friendly reception, hot showers, tropical garden with hammocks and barbecue. Very popular with backpackers, constantly recommended.

$ El Faro I, 14 Av Sur 9 entre 9 y 11 Calle Pte, T2447-7787, www.hoteleselfaro.com. Clean rooms, good price.

$ La Libertad, near cathedral, 4 Calle Ote 2, T2441-2358. With bath, good-value budget choice, friendly, clean, helpful. Safe car park across the street, US$2 for 24 hrs.

$ La Posada del Rey, 10 Av Sur 71, between 13 and 15 Calle Pte, east side of Mercado Colón and 50 m from bus terminal, T2440-0787, hotellaposadadelrey@hotmail.com. Low prices and nice rooms, friendly and helpful owners. A good backpacker choice and recommended.

Ahuachapán *p39*
$$ Casa Blanca, 2 Av Norte y Calle Gerardo Barrios, T2443-1505. 2 good, clean rooms with a/c. Recommended. Owner's husband is a doctor.

$$ El Parador, Km 102.5 road to Guatemala, 1.5 km west of town, T2443- 0331. Hotel and

restaurant, a/c, good service, motel-style, relaxing. Helpful owner, Sr Nasser. Buses to border stop outside. Recommended.
$ San José, 6 Calle Pte, opposite the park, T2413-0033. Clean, friendly, with bath. Parking available.

Tacuba *p40*
$$ La Cabaña de Tacuba, 50 m west of Alcaldía, T2417-4332. Nice hotel with large park grounds, access to river and swimming pools, a/c, cable TV. Great food at restaurant.
$ Hostal de Mama y Papa, Barrio El Calvario, 1 Calle 1, T2417-4268, www.imposible tours.com. Home of the delightful González family, dorm and private rooms with private bath available; roof terrace, DVDs, Wi-Fi access, crazy ducks guard the garden. Excellent, cheap food. The son, Manolo, runs **El Imposible Tours**, one of the most adventurous and expert outfits in the country.

Apaneca *p40*
$$$ Santa Leticia, Carretera Sonsonate Km 86.5, south of Apaneca, T2433-0357, www.coffee.com.sv. Comfortable double rooms, decorated in locally carved wood. Solar-heated pool, gardens, live music on Sun, restaurant. Close to **Santa Leticia** archaeological site.
$$ Las Cabañas de Apaneca, T2433-0500, www.cabanasapaneca.com. 12 cabins in pleasant gardens, many with good views. More expensive with full board.
$$ Villas Suizas, at entrance to Apaneca, T2433-0193. Several log cabins with kitchen and living room. Lovely gardens.
$$-$ Las Orquídeas, Av Central Sur 4, T2433-0061. Clean rooms, accessible prices, centrally located. Also offer accommodation in a family home.

Laguna Verde
Hotel Laguna Verde Guest House
$$ Hotel Laguna Verde Guest House, T7859-2865, www.apanecasguesthouse. netfirms.com. A nice small domo house and a wood cabin located at the rim of a deep secondary crater with a spectacular view. Located 250 m from Laguna Verde and 3 km from Apaneca, a perfect departure point for hiking in the area. Micobuses serve the area several times a day; check current schedules.

Ataco *p41*
$$ Alicante Montaña, Km 93.5 Carretera Apaneca/Ataco, T2433-0175, www.alicante apaneca.com. 26 very clean log-cabin rooms with hot water, cable TV. Huge, barnlike restaurant, good service and good value meals, pool, spa and jacuzzi; nice grounds with aviary. Very friendly and helpful. Recommended.
$$ El Jardín de Celeste, Km 94, Carretera Apaneca/Ataco, T2433-0277, www.eljardinde celeste.com. 10 rustic cabins with local flair located in a coffee grove and surrounded by colourful plants. The restaurant has capacity for larger parties and conventions. Beautifully decorated throughout the place with antiques, orchids, plants and arts and crafts.
$$ La Posada de Don Oli, Ataco, a few kilometres west of Apaneca, T2450-5155, oogomezduarte@yahoo.com.mx. Hotel and restaurant in a colonial setting, owned by the local mayor, Oscar Gómez. Guides available for visits to the local sights.
$$ Las Flores de Eloisa, Km 92.5 Carr Apaneca/Ataco, T2433-0415. Small cabins located inside a plant nursery.

North of Santa Ana *p41*
$$ San José, Carretera Internacional Km 113, Metapán, near bus station, T2442-0556, www.hotleselsalvador.com. A/c, quiet, cable TV, safe parking, restaurant on ground floor.
$$ Villa Limón, T2442-0149, www.canopy villalimon.com. 30 mins' drive up very rough road (4WD only) northwest of Metapán. Cosy, clean rooms in wooden *cabañas*, and a campsite in beautiful mountainside location, with huge zip-wires over the pine

forests. Amazing views over Metapán, to lakes and volcanoes beyond. Full board, or bring your own food, advanced reservation essential; guided walks to nearby waterfalls, and horse-riding trips available. Recommended.

$ Hospedaje Central, 2 Av Norte y Calle 15 de Septiembre. Clean, friendly and popular, with bath.

⊘ Eating

Izalco p33
$$ Casa de Campo, across from Turicentro Atecozol, T2453-6530. The old *casco* of the *finca* **Cuyancúa** has been restored with beautiful gardens, making it a good spot for a meal (only open at weekends). The fish raised in the artificial lake is served in the restaurant. Horses available for hire.

$ Mariona, in the centre, T2453-6580. One of several *comedores*. They serve a 55-year-old recipe for *sopa de gallina* (Creole chicken soup) which is famous all over Izalco.

$ Restaurante El Cheles, located in the centre of Izalco with another branch out of town at Final Av Roberto Carillas, Calle La Violeta, Caserío Texcalito, T2453-5392, www.izalcoelcherlerestaurant.com. Owner Ricardo Salazar speaks English and can arrange escorted hikes and horse riding to Cerro Verde.

Sonsonate p33
$ Burger House Plaza, Pasaje Francisco Chacón. Open 0900-2000. Hamburgers, fried chicken with potato salad.

$ Doña Laura, located inside **Hotel Agape** (see Sleeping, above). Open 0730-2100. Highly recommended.

Salcoatitán and Juayúa p34
Each weekend the whole central plaza of Juayua is invaded by the Gastronomical Food Fair, grab a chair and a table if you can, the event attracts folks from far and near. During the week there are several other options.

Check www.juayua. com. for a complete list of hotels and restaurants in this area.

$ Baking Pizza, 2a Calle Ote y 4a Av Sur, Juayua, T2469-2356. Home-made pizza.

$ Comedor Laura's, 1 block from the park on 1 Av Sur, Juayúa, T2452-2098. Open daily 0700-2000. 'The best in town' according to one reader, serving *comida a la vista*.

$ La Terraza, on corner of the park, Juayúa. A café and convenience store with a tourist kiosk nearby.

$ Parque Restaurante La Colina, Km 82 on the turn-off between Juayúa and Salcoatitán, T2452-2916, old timer in the region, popular with families, also has hammocks for relaxation after the meal as well as cabins and horse rides for the kids.

$ Taquería La Guadalupana, Av Daniel Cordón Sur and 2a Calle Ote, Juayúa T2452-2195. Good Mexican food.

Cafés
Pastelería y Cafetería Festival, 4 Calle Pte and 1 Av Sur, T2452-2269. Bakery and coffee shop – try the *pastelitos de ciruela* (plum pie) or the traditional *semita*. Good view overlooking the park.

Santa Ana p38, map p39
Restaurants close quite early, between 2000 and 2100. *Comedores* are usually cheap and good value or try the food stalls beside the plaza or in front of the cathedral. Look for excellent pineapples in season.

$$ Los Horcones, on main plaza next to the cathedral. Like a jungle lodge inside, with pleasant balcony dining, good cheap meals.

$$ Lover's Steak House, 4 Av Sur y 17 Calle Pte, T2440-5717. Great value, recommended.

$$ Talitunal, 5 Av Sur 6. Mon-Sat 0900-1900. Vegetarian, attractive, good lunch, owner is a doctor and expert on medicinal plants.

$ Expresión, 11 Calle Pte 20, between Av 6 and 8, T2440-1410, www.expresioncultural. org. A great little coffee bar, restaurant, bookshop and internet café, with occasional art exhibitions. The owner, Angel, speaks English. An obligatory stop. Recommended.

Chalchuapa *p38*
Several cheap and informal eateries with good-quality meals can be found around charming Parque Central.
$$ Los Antojitos, Calle Ramón Flores 6. Good meals.

Ahuachapán *p39*
There are now a handful of restaurants with lake views by Laguna del Espino just outside Ahuachapán.
$$ Restaurant El Paseo, **Restaurant Tanya** and **El Parador**, on the Las Chinamas road. All serve good meals.

Apaneca *p40*
Stalls in the municipal market offer cheap meals and typical dishes. Try the *budín* at the middle stall on the right side of market entrance (might be the best in El Salvador). A definite must for those on a budget or for experiencing local food.
$$$-$$ La Cocina de Mi Abuela, in town, T2433-0100, open weekends; and **Cabañas de Apaneca**. The 2 largest restaurants, and the most popular spots. Attract people from far and wide.
$$ El Rosario, by the turn-off at Km 95 between Apaneca and Ataco, T2433-0205, www.negociosyturismoelrosario.com. Offers grilled dishes, from regular *churrascos* to *pelibuey* (a mix between goat and sheep), *jaripeo* (Salvadorean version of rodeo), horse shows and musical entertainments weekends.
$$ Entre Nubes, Km 93.5, T2433-0345, exceptionally beautiful nursery plants surround this fine coffee shop (open weekends) great desserts and varieties of coffee.

$$ Parque Ecoturístico Las Cascadas de Don Juan, T2273-1380, lascascadasdedon juan@yahoo.com. Serving typical dishes and also offer hikes to the waterfalls, freshwater springs as well as a camping area.
$ Artesanías y Comedor Rosita. Range of local dishes as well as arts and crafts.
$ Laguna Verde Restaurant. Km 3.5 Carr El Caserío by La Laguna Verde, T2261-0167. A cosy and rustic spot serving typical dishes of the region. Only open weekends.

Ataco *p41*
A number of small restaurants and coffee shops have opened recently, most are only open at weekends.
$$-$ The House of Coffee, T2450-5353, thoc@hotmail.com. Tue-Sun. A must visit, the café has the only professional espresso machine in town. Home-made cakes and steaming hot 'Cup of Excellence' award-winning coffee is available here.
$$-$ Tayua, T7233-6508. A gem of a place 2 blocks uphill from the plaza, run by English-speaking and trained chef Veronica, and her husband. Wide range of dishes usually home-produced organic veg from the restaurant's own garden. Antique decor and background jazz. They also have a bakery, producing the best bread and pastries in town.

North of Santa Ana *p41*
Just before entering Metapán, 50 m off the highway, at the rim of the Lagunita Metapán, there are a couple of places with an inter-national menu offering good fish from the lake, including **La Cocina de Metapán**, T2423-0014, which also has a pool and terrace. Both have a/c.
$$-$ Balompie, Metapán, opposite church on main square, T2402-3567. Upstairs restaurant, nice balcony, serves good-value mix of meat, seafood, pasta and snacks. Also serves football stadium behind.

▲ Activities and tours

Ahuachapán p39
Tour operators
Tours Universales, at **Agencia de Viajes Morales**, 2 Av Norte 2-4, T2413-2002. Speak to Beatriz Contreras.

Tacuba p40
El Imposible Tours, see **Hostal de Mama y Papa**, page 44. Range of activities including mountain biking, canyoning and hiking; overnight trips combining tour of Barra de Santiago and mangroves. Highly recommended.

Apaneca p40
Tour operators
Apaneca Aventura, Calle Los Platanares 2, T2433-0470, apanecaaventura@yahoo.com. Specialize in off-road buggy rides around the mountains and forests, including to Laguna Verde and Ausole de Santa Teresa geysers and thermal baths. English manager Becky, and with English-speaking guides. Highly recommended.

☺ Transport

Sonsonate p33
Bus No 248 to **Santa Ana**, US$1.50 along Carr 12 north, 39 km, a beautiful journey. To **Ahuachapán**, bus No 249, 2 hrs, slow, best to go early in the day. To Ataco, via Juayúa and Ahuachapán, No 23, US$1, 1½ hrs To **Barra de Santiago**, bus No 285. To **Los Cobanos** bus No 259. Take care at the bus terminal and on rural routes (eg in Nahuizalco area). From **San Salvador** to Sonsonate by bus No 530, US$0.80, 1½ hrs, very frequent.

Joya de Cerén p36
Bus No 108 from **San Salvador** Terminal de Occidente to San Juan; US$0.45, 1 hr. Bus No 201 from **Santa Ana**, US$0.60, 1 hr, ask the bus driver to drop you at Desvío Opico from where you can catch another bus to Joya de Cerén.

Lago de Coatepeque p36
Bus From **Santa Ana**, bus No 220 'El Lago' to the lake every 30 mins, US$0.35. From **San Salvador**; bus No 201 to El Congo (bridge at Km 50) on Pan-American Hwy, US$1, then pick up the No 220 bus to the lake, US$0.45. Other buses to **Guatemala** may also stop at El Congo, so it's worth checking.

Taxi From Santa Ana, US$10.

Cerro Verde and Volcán Izalco p37
Bus From **Santa Ana**, bus No 248 goes to Santa Ana and Cerro Verde via El Congo. If you come from San Salvador wait for the bus at the other side of the main road, near the turn-off to Lake Coatepeque. The departures from Santa Ana are 0800, 1000 1100 and 1300. The bus arrives approximately 30 mins later at El Congo. The return bus leaves Cerro Verde at 1100, 1200, 1300, 1500, 1600 and 1730. The latest bus stops at El Congo and does not go all the way to Santa Ana. The journey between Cerro Verde at El Congo takes approximately 1 hr.

If you travel from **San Salvador** take the bus towards Santa Ana (No 205). Get off at the Shell gas station at El Congo, cross the bridge that goes over the highway and catch the No 248 at the junction from Santa Ana. If you come from the west take the bus from Esso gas station beween Izalco and Ateos that leads to Santa Ana and get off at junction 14 km below Cerro Verde summit and wait for No 248 that comes from El Congo.

Santa Ana p38, map p39
Bus No 201 from Terminal del Occidente, **San Salvador**, US$1-1.25, 1 hr, every 10-15 mins, 0400-1830. To **La Libertad**, take 'autopista' route bus to San Salvador and change buses in Nueva San Salvador. Buses (**Melva**, **Pezzarossi** and others) leave frequently from 25 Calle Pte y 8 Av Sur, T2440-3606, for **Guatemala City**, full fare as from San Salvador, 4-4½ hrs including border

stops. Alternatively, there are local buses to the border for US$0.45; they leave from the market. Frequent buses to **Metapán** and border at **Anguiatú**. No 238 follows a beautiful route to **Juayúa**.

Atiquizaya *p39*
Bus There are frequent buses to the river from the central park in Atiquizaya; buses No 202 and 456 from Terminal Occidente in **San Salvador**, 2 hrs, US$0.90. From **Santa Ana**, 45 mins, US$0.40. All Ahuachapán buses stop in the Parque Central.

Ahuachapán *p39*
Bus Ahuachapán is 100 km from **San Salvador** by bus 202, US$0.90, every 20 mins, 0430-1830 to the capital, 2 hrs via **Santa Ana**. Microbuses to border from northwest corner of parque, US$0.45, 25 mins, slower buses same price. Bus No 210 to **Santa Ana** 1 hr, US$0.50. Bus No 235 El Express to **Metapán** 1¼ hrs, US$0.90. Frequent buses and minivans to the border at Km 117.

Tacuba *p40*
Bus Buses leave the terminal in **Ahuachapán** every 30 mins, 0500-1530, return 1630-1700, via **Ataco**; US$0.60, 45 mins, rough road.

Apaneca *p40*
Bus Local buses stop by the plaza, others pass on the main road, a few blocks north, leaving you with a fairly long walk. **Laguna Verde** can be reached on foot from Apaneca

to Cantón Palo Verde and Hoyo de Cuajuste, then a further 1 km from where the road ends.

North of Santa Ana *p41*
Bus and car From Santa Ana bus No 235, US$0.80, 1 hr. If driving **San Salvador**–Metapán, a bypass skirts Santa Ana. Bus No 211 to border at **Anguiatú**.

ℹ Directory

Salcoatitán, Juayúa, Ahuachapán and Ataco *p34, p39 and p41*
Banks **Scotia Bank** (with ATM), Juayúa, opposite bus stop from Ahuachapan. Mon-Fri 0800-1600, Sat 0800-1200. There are several banks in Sonsonate and Ahuachapán. Ataco has Pro Credit and Western Union banks, 1 block from main square, both with ATMs. **Internet** Mini Librería, 4 Calle Ote, ½ block from main square, Juayúa. **Post** 1 block from main square, Ataco, towards market, 0900-1630.

Santa Ana *p38, map p39*
Banks Banks will change TCs, though becoming less widely accepted. **HSBC** and several other banks, Av Independencia Sur, between Calle 3 and 7. **Internet** Expresión, has a couple of computers on the go in a very comfortable setting. **Laundry** Lavandería Solución, 7 Calle Pte 29, wash and dry US$2.50 per load, ironing service, recommended. **Police** Emergency T911. **Post** 7 Calle Pte, between 2 Av and Av Independencia Sur.

Northern El Salvador

The route from San Salvador to western Honduras heads north, skirting the vast arm of the Cerrón Grande reservoir with volcanoes in the distance. Small villages are interspersed with brand new settlements tucked amongst the fields and hills as the road winds through mountainous landscape – a snapshot of the old way of life, and the emergence of the new. Currently enjoying a cultural revival, the charming colonial town of Suchitoto on the southern shore of the reservoir is definitely worth a visit.

North from San Salvador → *For listings, see pages 53-56.*

The old highway, Troncal del Norte (CA 4) used to be the only acess to the north from the capital, but has been replaced with a modern highway. This can be accessed from Boulevard de la Constitución, in the northeastern part of San Salvador, and swirls west around the Volcán de San Salvador towards the Pan-American Highway and branches out to Nejapa, Quezaltepeque and Apopa to the north. Another advance in the northern road system is the road that connects Aguilares with Suchitoto. It is 2½ hours by car from San Salvador to La Palma, then 11 km to the border at El Poy.

Apopa and Tonacatepeque
ⓘ *Bus 38 B from San Salvador to Apopa, US$0.35.*
Apopa is a friendly town with a good market and a shopping centre. It is the junction with a road to Quezaltepeque (12 km). A paved road runs east from Apopa to Tonacatepeque, an attractive small town on a high plateau. It has a small textile industry and is in an agricultural setting – check out the charming park and the colonial church. There has been some archaeological exploration of the town's original site, 5 km away. A paved road from Tonacatepeque runs 13 km south to the Pan-American Highway, some 5 km from the capital. In the other direction, a dry-weather road runs north to Suchitoto. Three kilometres beyond Apopa, on CA 4 Km 17, is **Finca Orgánica Las Termópilas** where Lisa's **Guest House** is located (see page 53). There is also a Spanish-language school and they arrange volunteers for the 'Working Farm' project at Termópilas organic farm. Tours are available to the archaeological site Cihuatán (see below) as well as on horseback to Suchitoto and to Volcán Guazapa, which played a prominent part in the civil war. The panoramic views are amazing and you can visit the old guerrilla hide outs. Contact Lena and René Carmona at **Ximena's** (see page 25), T2260-2481. All buses from Terminal de Oriente to Aguilares pass the entrance (US$0.25).

Aguilares
From Apopa, it's 21 km to Aguilares, 4 km beyond which are the ruins of **Cihuatán**
ⓘ *Tue-Sun 0900-1600, map of the site with the Sendero Interpretativo is available from Lisa's*

Guest House or Ximena's Guest House; alternatively, contact chief archaeologist Paul Amaroli *at FUNDAR in San Salvador, T2235-9453, www.fundar.org.sv.* The name means 'place of women' and was presided over by female royalty. This was the largest city in Mesoamerica during the Toltec period, when the city was surrounded by extended fortification measuring more than 10 sq km. The biggest archaeological site in the country has several tall pyramids, ball courts and *temazcales* (ritual saunas).

An improved road goes from Aguilares heading west to Suchitoto. If heading north, see page 53.

Suchitoto → *Population: 24,786. For listings, see pages 53-56.*

ⓘ *Good sites on Suchitoto are www.gaesuchitoto.com and www.suchitoto-el-salvador.com. For information in English, try to contact US citizen Roberto Broz who runs a Cyber Café Store and Restaurant El Gringo, just off the main plaza, see Eating, page 55.*

Suchitoto, meaning 'the place of birds and flowers' in Náhuatl, was founded by the Pipil more than 1000 years ago. In 1528 the capital was moved to Suchitoto for 15 years as the villa of San Salvador suffered attacks from local tribes. In 1853 an earthquake destroyed much of San Salvador and many affluent families moved to Suchitoto leaving a lasting impression on the town. Today it is a small, very attractive colonial town with cobbled streets, balconied houses and an interesting church. It is one of the favourite tourist spots in the country, with cultural traditions kept alive by the many artists living and working in the town. Several hotels and restaurants offer fantastic views towards Suchitlán and

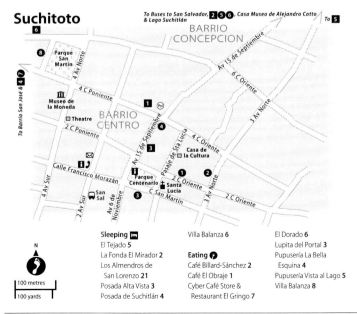

Suchitoto

Sleeping 🛏
El Tejado **5**
La Fonda El Mirador **2**
Los Almendros de
  San Lorenzo **21**
Posada Alta Vista **3**
Posada de Suchitlán **4**
Villa Balanza **6**

Eating 🍴
Café Billard-Sánchez **2**
Café El Obraje **1**
Cyber Café Store &
  Restaurant El Gringo **7**

El Dorado **6**
Lupita del Portal **3**
Pupusería La Bella
  Esquina **4**
Pupusería Vista al Lago **5**
Villa Balanza **8**

Volcán Guazapa. More than 200 species of bird have been identified in the area, and white-tailed deer inhabit the local woods.

The town was almost completely deserted in the early 1990s after 12 years of civil war which severely affected the region – 90% of the population left, leaving Suchitoto a virtual ghost town. However, a cultural revival has stimulated a range of activities and events, and the town is now considered the cultural capital of the country. Life centres on the main plaza which every evening becomes a bustle of people wandering the streets. Suchitoto's telegraph poles have been decorated by artist Paulo Rusconi, and Parque San Martín, to the west of town, is dotted with modern sculptures, some made using materials left over from the war. Arts and cultural festivals with internationally renowned artists take place every February. Another local festivity is the *Palo Encebado*, a competition involving attempts to clamber to the top of long greasy poles, and the *cerdo encebado* where a pig smeared with lard is chased through town and is kept by the first person who manages to grab it.

The **Teatro de Las Ruinas** is almost fully restored and hosts concerts and events. Contact Sra Chavez, T2335-1086 for more information. **Iglesia de Santa Lucía** ① *Mon-Sat 0800-1200, 1400-1600, all day Sun*, built in 1858 with wooden and hollow columns, has also been restored with a lot of stencil work inside. There is a splendid view from the church tower. **Casa Museo de Alejandro Cotto** ① *daily 0900-1200 and 1400-1600, US$4, guided tour in Spanish (T2335-1140)*, home of movie director Alejandro Cotto, is an interesting museum with more than 132 paintings of El Salvador's most renowned artists, collections of books and music instruments.

The **tourist office** ① *Calle Francisco Morazán 7, next to the telephone office, T2335-1782, daily 0800-1700, www.suchitoto-el-salvador.com*, offers daily tours of the city centre, to Los Tercios waterfall and to Lake Suchitlán. There is also a Ministry of Tourism **tourist office** ① *Mon-Fri 0800-1700, Sat-Sun 0800-1600, T2335-1835,* in Suchitoto.

Around Suchitoto

A 30-minute walk north of town leads to the **Embalse Cerrón Grande** (also known as **Lago de Suchitlán**). **Proyecto Turístico Pesquero Puerto San Juan** is the a harbour with boat shuttle services and a complex of, restaurants, craft shops and cafés on the lake shore. This is the departure point for boat excursions across to remote areas in neighbouring Chalatenango, ask around and negotiate prices. Trips are available to five islands including **Isla de Los Pájaros**, which makes an interesting trip (one to 1½ hours).

Ferries cross the Embalse Cerrón Grande for San Luis del Carmen (25 minutes to San Luis, frequent departures all day), where there is Comedor Carmen, and buses to Chalatenango. The ferry also makes a stop at the small village of **San Francisco Lempa**.

Los Tercios, a waterfall with striking, gigantic, black, hexagonal-shaped basaltic columns, can be reached by car, foot and by *lancha*. It is at its most impressive in the wet season when the full force of nature is on show. Walk 10-15 minutes from town down the very steep road towards the lake known as Calle al Lago de Suchitlán. Lifts are available for about US$2-3 if you can't face the steep climb back to town afterwards, ask around. At the lake shore, where there are *comedores*, ask for a *lanchero*. A *lancha* to the base of the trail to Los Tercios is US$5-6 (negotiable) and takes 10 minutes (ask the *lanchero* to point out the trail).

La Ciudad Vieja, one-time site of the capital, is 10 km from Suchitoto. An original Pipil town, it was taken over by the Spanish who made it their central base for 17 years before electrical storms, lack of water, and cholera forced them to flee. It is a private site but can be visited. There are plans for a museum and a café.

Handicrafts of El Salvador

The artists' village of **La Palma**, in a pine-covered valley under Miramundo mountain, is 84 km north of the capital 10 km south of the Honduran frontier. Here, in 1971, the artist **Fernando Llort** 'planted a seed' known as the *copinol* (a species of the locust tree) from which sprang the first artists' cooperative, now called **La Semilla de Dios** (Seed of God). The copinol seed is firm and round; on it the artisans base a spiritual motif that emanates from their land and soul.

The town and its craftspeople are now famous for their work in wood, including exotically carved *cofres* (adorned wooden chests), and traditional Christmas *muñecas de barro* (clay dolls) and ornamental angels. Wood carvings, other crafts and the designs of the original paintings by Llort, are all produced and exported from La Palma to the rest of El Salvador and thence worldwide.

In 1971 the area was almost exclusively agricultural. Today 75% of the population of La Palma and neighbouring San Ignacio are engaged directly or indirectly in producing handicrafts. The painter **Alfredo Linares** (born 1957 in Santa Ana, arrived in La Palma 1981 after studying in Guatemala and Florence) has a gallery in La Palma, employing and assisting local artists. His paintings and miniatures are marketed abroad, yet you will often find him working in the family pharmacy next to the gallery. Many of La Palma's images are displayed on the famous Hilasal towels. If you cannot get to La Palma, visit the shop/gallery/workshop of Fernando Llort in San Salvador, **Arbol de Dios**.

Twenty kilometres from the capital is the indigenous town of **Panchimalco**, where weaving on the loom and other traditional crafts are being revived. Many Náhuatl traditions, customs, dances and the language survived here as the original indigenous people hid from the Spanish conquistadors in the valley beneath the Puerta del Diablo (now in Parque Balboa). In 1996 the painter Eddie Alberto Orantes and his family opened the **Centro de Arte y Cultura Tunatiuh**, named after a Náhuatl deity who is depicted as a human face rising as a sun over a pyramid. The project employs local youths (from broken homes, or former addicts) in the production of weavings, paintings and ceramics.

In the mountains of western El Salvador, villages in the coffee zone, such as **Nahuizalco**, specialize in weaving henequen, bamboo and reed into table mats and wicker furniture. There are also local artists like Maya sculptor **Ahtzic Selis**, who works with clay and jade. East of the capital, at **Ilobasco** (60 km), many ceramic workshops produce items including the famous *sorpresas*, miniature figures enclosed in an egg shell. In the capital there are craft markets, and throughout the country, outlets range from the elegant to the rustic. Everywhere, artists and artisans welcome visitors into their workshops.

Boat trips go to lakeside villages associated with the FMLN in the civil war. On the road to Aguilares, 12 km away, a **Bosque de la Reconciliación** is being developed at the foot of Cerro de Guazapa. Contact **CESTA** ① *T2213-1400, www.cesta-foe.org*, in San Salvador, or contact the park directly on T2213-1403 and speak to Jesús Arriola. Also, 3 km along this road is **Aguacayo** and a large church, badly damaged during the war.

Chalatenango → *Altitude: 450 m. Population: 30,808. For listings, see pages 53-56.*

Highway 4 continues north from **Aguilares**, passing the western extremity of the **Cerrón Grande** reservoir. A branch to the east skirts the northern side of the reservoir to Chalatenango, capital of the department of the same name. Chalatenango is a delightful little town with annual fairs and fiestas on 24 June and 1-2 November. It is the centre of an important region of traditional livestock farms. It has a good market and several craft shops, for example **Artesanías Chalateca**, for bags and hammocks. The weekly horse fairs, where horses, saddles and other equipment are for sale, are very popular.

La Palma and around → *Altitude: 1100 m. Population: 12,235. For listings, see pages 53-56.*

The main road continues north through Tejutla to La Palma, a charming village set in pine-clad mountains, and well worth a visit. It is famous for its local crafts, particularly brightly painted wood carvings and hand-embroidered tapestries. Also produced are handicrafts made from clay, metal, cane and seeds. There are a number of workshops in La Palma where the craftsmen can be seen at work and purchases made (see box, page 52). The **Fiesta del Dulce Nombre de María** takes place mid- or late-February.

The picturesque village of **San Ignacio**, 6 km north of La Palma, has two or three small *talleres* producing handicrafts (20 minutes by bus, US$0.10 each way).

San Ignacio is the departure point for buses ascending a fairly new, safe but steep road leading up to the highest mountain of El Salvador, El Pital (2730 m). As you reach the pass below the mountain top, the road branches to **Las Pilas** to the left and **Miramundo** to the right. Both Miramundo and Las Pilas have small agricultural communities, specializing in organic crops. The extensive cabbage fields combined with the pine-clad mountains make for beautiful vistas. If you take the road from the summit to the right, you end up in Miramundo which gives a view of pretty much all El Salvador. On clear days you can see almost all the volcanoes in the country, including Volcán Pacaya and Volcán Agua in Guatemala. No doubt the best view in the country.

Border with Western Honduras
The road continues north to the border at **El Poy**, for Western Honduras. From Citalá, there is a small town with a colonial church and a potent war history (you still see bullet holes in the walls of the houses on street corners). One kilometre west off the highway just before El Poy, an adventurous road leads to Metapán. Two buses daily take three hours to travel the 40 km, a rough but beautiful journey.

Northern El Salvador listings

For Sleeping and Eating price codes and other relevant information, see page 10.

🛏 Sleeping

Apopa and Tonacatepeque *p49*
$ Lisa's Guest House, Finca Orgánica Las Termópilas, 3 km beyond Apopa, on CA 4 Km 17.5, Troncal del Norte, www.ximenas guesthouse.com. Same owners as **Ximena's Guest House**, T2260-2481, in San Salvador, see page 25. Budget lodging in dorms with shared bath, and spacious family rooms with TV and private bath.

Suchitoto *p50, map p50*

$$$$ Los Almendros de San Lorenzo, 4 Calle Pte, next to police station, T2335-1200, www.hotelsalvador.com. In a restored colonial house with exclusive rooms, suites and delightful gardens. Delicious meals in the restaurant – people come from the capital to lunch here at weekends. Art Gallery **Pascal**, across the street, has great exhibits, textiles and handicrafts (same French owner).

$$$$-$$$ Posada de Suchitlán, Final 4 Calle Pte, at the western end of town, T2335-1064, www.laposada.com.sv. Colonial-style, beautifully tiled and decorated, excellent hotel and restaurant, including local speciality, *gallo a chichi* (chicken cooked in maize wine); stunning lake views.

$$$-$$ El Tejado, 3 Av Norte 58, Barrio Concepción, T2335-1769, www.eltejado suchitoto.net. Beautifully restored colonial house with just nicely furnished and spotless rooms, some with balcony; pool and gorgeous view of Lake Suchitlán. Pretty terrace restaurant.

$$ Hacienda La Bermuda 1525, Km 34.8 Carretera a Suchitoto, T2226-1839, www.labermuda.com. Hotel and restaurant with frequent cultural activities, located just outside Suchitoto.

$$ Villa Balanza, north edge of Parque San Martín, T2335-1408, www.villabalanza restaurante.com. On the street behind the restaurant of the same name and 250 m to the right down the hill. Small rooms but nicely furnished, with lovely views of lake from the hotel balcony.

$$-$ Posada Alta Vista, on Av 15 de Septiembre 8, near the square, T2335-1645. Good rooms, although the cheaper ones can be hot. Helpful, friendly staff. Rooftop terrace with great view of the town.

$ La Fonda El Mirador, Calle 15 de Septiembre, Barrio Concepción, on the road that leads to the lake, T2335-1126, quintanilladavid@yahoo.com. Next to restaurant of same name, with superb views of lake and good food too.

Chalatenango *p53*

$ La Ceiba, 1a calle Pte, near 5a Av Norte, behind the military fort, Barrio Las Flores, T2301-1080. With shower and bath. Basic rooms but with a/c, in quiet corner of town.

La Palma and around *p53*

$$$ Entre Pinos, San Ignacio, T2335-9312, www.entrepinosresortandspa.com. 1st-class resort complex, a/c, pool, cable TV, sauna and small shop.

$$ Hotel La Palma, Troncal del Norte, 84 km Carretera, La Palma, T2335-9012, www.hotellapalma.com.sv. 32 large rooms, clean, with bath. Friendly, with good restaurant, beautiful gardens, nice pool, ceramics workshop, parking and gas station. Also runs guided walks around local trails, including El Tecomate, Río Nunuapa and Los Pozos. Recommended.

$$ Hotel Maya, Km 77.5 Troncal del Norte, T2323-3758. Motel at the entrance of La Palma. Amazing panoramic view.

$$ La Posada de Reyes, San Ignacio, just behind the park, T2352-9223. Nice private rooms with bath, also has a restaurant.

$ Casa de Huéspedes Las Orquídeas, Las Pilas. Run by a local farming family – ask for a guided trip to the mountain top nearby, for an unrivalled panoramic view and free peaches.

$ Hostal Miramundo, Miramundo, T2219-6251, www.hotelmiramundo.com. Nice rooms with hot water. A restaurant, great food and great views. Recommended.

$ Hotel Cayahuanca, San Ignacio, across the street at Km 93.5, T2335-9464. Friendly, with good but expensive restaurant.

$ Las Praderas de San Ignacio, San Ignacio, a couple of kilometres before the border, T2350-9330, www.hotelpraderas desanignacio.com. Cabins, beautiful gardens and an economic restaurant.

Apopa and Tonacatepeque *p49*

$$ La Posada de John Paul, Finca Orgánica Las Termópilas. Serves food made with own-grown produce, as well as meat dishes and natural fruit juices. Excellent organic honey and coffee available, and fruit and vegetables when in season.

Suchitoto *p50, map p50*

Local specialities include *salporitas* (made of corn meal) and *chachamachas*. Try the *pupusas* in the market. Several eating options around the main plaza; many restaurants only open weekend evenings, especially during off season.

$$$ Los Almendros de San Lorenzo, 4 Calle Pte, next to police station, Barrio El Centro (see Sleeping), T2335-1200, plebailly@hotelelsalvador.com. Best restaurant in Suchitoto. Has a French chef, serves succulent meals and visitors come from San Salvador on weekends to dine here.

$$ El Dorado, by Lake Suchitlán, T2225-5103, www.gaesuchitoto.com. Bar and restaurant that hosts frequent concerts.

$$ Hacienda La Bermuda, just out of Suchitoto, Km 34.8 Carretera a San Salvador (see Sleeping), T2389-9078, www.labermuda.com. B&B, colonial-style restaurant with pool and cultural events.

$$ Lupita del Portal, Parque Centenario, T2335-1679. The current hot spot, open until midnight. Serves gourmet *pupusas* with home-grown herbs, Salvadorean specialities and natural teas. Owner René Barbón also runs **Suchitoto Adventure Outfitters** (T2335-1429) from here, an excellent tour operator (see below).

$$ Villa Balanza, Parque San Martín, T2335-1408, www.villabalanzarestaurante.com. Rustic farm decor and antique bric-a-brac, serving excellent local cuisine, steaks and fish, and home-made fruit preserves.

$$ Vista Conga Restaurant, T2335-1679, Final Pasaje Cielito Lindo No 8 Barrio

Concepción, vistacongasuchi@yahoo.com. Live music, only open at weekends.

$ Café Billard-Sánchez, 4 Calle Pte, by El Cerrito, Barrio Santa Lucía, T2335-1464. Bar and disco.

$ Café El Obraje, next to Santa Lucía church, T2335-1173. Clean and reasonably priced, with good breakfast variety. Closed Tue.

$ Cyber Café Store and Restaurant El Gringo, T2335-1770, 8a Av Norte No 9, Barrio San José. Fri-Wed. Serves *pupusas* (normal and gourmet), Tex/Mex and typical Salvadorean foods. Famous for veggie burritos.

$ Pupusería La Bella Esquina, on 15 de Septiembre and 4 Calle Ote. Very good, cheap food.

$ Pupusería Vista al Lago, Av 15 de Septiembre 89, T2335-1134. Good food.

Chalatenango *p53*

Several restaurants to choose from including:

$$$-$ Rinconcito El Nuevo, next to the military fort. A la carte menu as well as *pupusas*, good. Check out bizarre collection of old sewing machines, irons, typewriters and other knick-knacks on display in the adjacent colonnade.

La Palma and around *p53*

In Ignacio, there are many local *comedores*, including **Comedor Elisabeth**, which offer delicious *comida a la vista* including fresh milk, cheese and cream.

$ El Poyeton, Barrio San Antonio, 1 block from church, La Palma. Reliable, serves simple dishes.

$ La Estancia, on Calle Principal, La Palma, T2335-9049. Open 0800-2000. Good menu, useful bulletin board.

▲ Activities and tours

Suchitoto *p50, map p50*

Suchitoto Adventure Outfitters, based in **Lupita del Portal** café on main square, T2335-1429, www.suchitotooutfitters.com. Excellent local tours, including 5-hr horse-riding trip up Volcán Guazapa to former guerrilla camp, fascinating insights on war history (US$35). Owner René Barbón speaks excellent English and is extremely knowledgeable and helpful.

◉ Shopping

La Palma and around *p53*
Handicrafts

There are more than 80 arts and crafts workshops in La Palma, www.lapalma elsalvador.com, provides a complete list of all the workshops and how to contact them. Many workshops have come together and formed a **Placita Artesanal** – an artisans market, which is located by the Catholic church on the central plaza.

Cooperativa La Semilla de Dios, Plaza San Antonio. The original cooperative founded by Fernando Llort in 1971, it has a huge selection of crafts and paintings, helpful.

Gallery Alfredo Linares, Sr Linares' house (if gallery is unattended, ask in the pharmacy), T2335-9049. Open daily 0900-1800. Well-known artist whose paintings sell for US$18-75, friendly, recommended.

Palma City, Calle Principal behind church. Sra Alicia Mata is very helpful and will help find objects, whether she stocks them or not (wood, ceramics, *telas*, etc).

◉ Transport

Suchitoto *p50, map p50*
Bus To **Aguilares**, No 163 every 30 mins, 0500-1800, 30 mins. Regular buses (No 129) from Terminal Oriente, **San Salvador**, beginning at 0330. The bus stops at the market and leaves town for the capital from 3 Av Norte. To **Ilobasco** by dirt road, 0800 and 1000, returning 1230 and 1430.

Ferry Cross the Embalse Cerrón Grande (Lago de Suchitlán) for **San Luis del**

Carmen (25 mins to San Luis, frequent departures throughout the day, will leave whenever full, cars US$8, foot passengers US$1) where there is **Comedor Carmen**, and buses linking to **Chalatenango**. Small *lanchas* also make the short crossing from San Juan to San Francisco Lempa on the north shore, with onward buses to Chalatenango, US$5 for the whole boat (up to approximately 10 passengers).

Chalatenango *p53*
Bus No 125 from Oriente terminal, **San Salvador**, US$2, 2½ hrs.

La Palma and around *p53*
Bus From **San Salvador**, Terminal de Oriente, No 119, US$2.25, 3 hrs, last bus at 1630. To La Palma from Amayo, crossroads with Troncal del Norte (main highway to San Salvador), and east–west road to Chalatenango, bus No 119 every 30 mins, US$1.35.

◉ Directory

Suchitoto *p50, map p50*
Banks Western Union available. Mon-Fri 0800-1600, Sat 0830-1200. Will cash TCs. No credit card facilities. **Internet** Cyber Café El Gringo, daily 0800-2100, US$1per hr, free Wi-Fi for laptops; Barrio San José; 2 places on the main square either side of **Lupita del Portal**.

Chalatenango *p53*
Banks HSBC and Banco Pro Credit on 3 Av Sur, **Western Union** off plaza to right of barracks, all with ATM.

La Palma and around *p53*
Banks Citibank, Calle Delgado and Av Independencia, with 24-hr ATM.

Eastern El Salvador

A primarily agricultural zone, the central region is lined with dramatic volcanoes, impressive scenery and the small towns of the Lempa Valley. Along the coast, quiet beaches and islands can be found on the way to the stunning Gulf of Fonseca to the east. In the north towards the mountain range bordering Honduras was an area of fierce disputes between the army and guerrillas during the civil war (1980-1992). Small communities are now rebuilt and opening up to visitors providing several small quaint villages offer ecotourism and original crafts. There are two border crossings to Honduras: to the north at Perquín, and the east at El Amatillo.

East from San Salvador → *For listings, see pages 63-66.*

There are two roads to the port of La Unión (formerly known as Cutuco) on the Gulf of Fonseca: the Pan-American Highway, 185 km through Cojutepeque and San Miguel (see page 59); and the coastal highway, also paved, running through Santo Tomás, Olocuilta, Zacatecoluca and Usulután.

The Pan-American Highway is dual carriageway out of the city, but becomes single carriageway for several kilometres either side of Cojutepeque – sections that are twisty, rough and seem to induce some very bad driving.

At San Martín, 18 km from the capital, a paved road heads north to Suchitoto, 25 km on the southern shore of the Embalse Cerrón Grande, also known as Lago de Suchitlán. At Km 34.8 is **Hacienda La Bermuda**, see page 54.

Cojutepeque → *Population: 50,315.*
The capital of the Department of Cuscatlán, 34 km from San Salvador, is the first town on the Pan-American Highway encountered when heading east. There is a good weekly market. The town is famous for cigars, smoked sausages, *quesadillas* and tongue, and its annual feria on 29 August has fruits and sweets, saddlery, leather goods, pottery and headwear on sale from neighbouring villages, and sisal hammocks, ropes, bags and hats from the small factories of Cacaopera (Department of Morazán). There is also a sugar cane festival on 12-20 January. Lago de Ilopango is a short trip to the southwest.

Cerro de las Pavas, a conical hill near Cojutepeque, dominates Lago de Ilopango and offers splendid views of wide valleys and tall mountains. Its shrine of **Our Lady of Fátima** draws many pilgrims every year (religious ceremonies take place here on 13 May).

Ilobasco → *Population 61,510.*
From **San Rafael Cedros**, 6 km east of Cojutepeque, a 16-km paved road north to Ilobasco has a branch road east to Sensuntepeque at about Km 13. The surrounding area, devoted

---

to cattle, coffee, sugar and indigo, is exceptionally beautiful. Many of Ilobasco's population are workers in clay; although some of its decorated pottery is now mass-produced and has lost much of its charm, this is definitely the best place to buy pottery in El Salvador. Check out miniature *sorpresas*, delicately shaped microscopic sceneries the size of an egg (don't miss the naughty ones). Try **Hermanos López**, at the entrance to town, or **José y Víctor Antino Herrera** ① *Av Carlos Bonilla 61, T2332-2324, look for the 'Kiko' sign*, where there are fine miniatures for sale. The annual fiesta is on 29 September.

San Sebastián → *Population 14,411.*

Four kilometres from the turning to Ilobasco, further south along the Pan-American Highway at **Santo Domingo** (Km 44 from San Salvador), a paved road leads for 5 km to San Sebastián, where colourfully patterned cloth hammocks and bedspreads are made. You can watch them being woven on complex looms of wood and string. Behind **Funeraria Durán** there is a weaving workshop. Sr Durán will take you past the caskets to see the weavers. The **Casa de Cultura**, about 50 m from the plaza, will direct you to weaving centres and give information on handicrafts. Before buying, check prices and beware of overcharging. Market day is on Monday.

San Vicente → *Population: 53,213.*

Founded in 1635, San Vicente is 61 km from the capital and lies a little southeast of the Highway on the Río Alcahuapa, at the foot of the double-peaked **Volcán San Vicente** (or

San Vicente

Sleeping ▦
Central Park 2

Eating ◉
Acapulco 1
Comedor Rivolí 2

Chinchontepec), with very fine views of the Jiboa valley to the west. The town enjoys a lovely setting and is a peaceful place to spend a night or two. Its pride and joy is **El Pilar** (1762-1769), the most original church in the country. It was here that the local chief, **Anastasio Aquino**, took the crown from the statue of San José and crowned himself King of the Nonualcos during the rebellion of 1832.

El Pilar stands on a small square 1½ blocks south of the Parque Central. On the latter is the **cathedral**, whose nave is draped with golden curtains. In the middle of the main plaza is a tall, open-work **clock tower**, quite a landmark when descending the hill into the city. Three blocks east of the main plaza is the *tempisque* tree under which the city's foundation charter was drawn up. The tree was decreed a national monument on 26 April 1984. There's an extensive market area a few blocks west of the centre and hammock sellers are on nearby streets. An army barracks takes up an entire block in the centre. There's a small **war museum**; ask the FMLN office here or in San Salvador. Carnival day is 1 November.

Around San Vicente

Three kilometres southeast of the town is the **Balneario Amapulapa** ① *T2393-0412, US$0.80 entry and US$0.90 parking charges, a Turicentro*. There are three pools at different levels in a wooded setting. The tourist police patrols here and lately it's been considered a safe place for tourists, although women should not walk to the area alone. Reached by bus No 177 from Zacatecoluca bus station, and by pickup from the San Vicente Bus station. **Laguna de Apastepeque** ① *T2389-7172*, near San Vicente off the Pan-American Highway, is small but picturesque. Take bus No 156 from San Vicente, or 499 from San Salvador. Ask in San Vicente for guides for climbing the San Vicente volcano.

San Miguel → *Population: 218,410.*

Set at the foot of the **Volcán San Miguel** (**Chaparrastique**), which last erupted in 1976 but has shown activity ever since, San Miguel is the third largest city in El Salvador, 136 km from San Salvador. The capital of its Department, the town was founded in 1530 as a military fortress by Don Luis de Moscoso. It now has one of the fastest growing economies in Central America, has two shady plazas: **Parque David J Guzmán**, containing the bare 18th-century cathedral, and the adjacent **Plaza Barrios**, flanked by overflowing market stalls. The city's **theatre** dates from 1909, but since the 1960s it has been used for various purposes other than the arts. After several years of restoration it reopened in 2003 in all its original glory. There is a Metrocentro shopping centre southeast of the centre, on Avenida Roosevelt Sur and the **Turicentro of Altos de la Cueva** ① *T2669-0699*, is 1 km north (take bus No 94 in front of the cathedral in San Miguel, US$0.80). It offers swimming pools, gardens, restaurants, sports facilities and bungalows for rent (US$34), and is busy at weekends.

The arid climate all year round makes the region ideal for growing maize, beans, cotton and sisal, and some silver and gold are mined here. However, the biggest industry is the *remesas* (money received from family members who have emigrated to the US), as this part of the country experienced heavy migration both during and after the civil war.

The fiesta de la Virgen de la Paz is on the last Saturday in November, and one of the biggest carnivals in Central America, known as *El Carnaval de San Miguel*, also takes place here. The free festival features parades and marching bands filing down Avenida Roosevelt to the city centre, from 1900 until late. For more information contact the

Comité de Festejos ① *T2660-1326*. Apart from this event, San Miguel is not a place you're likely to want to linger; thee are traffic-clogged streets, stinking gutters, a hot, sticky climate and few conventional tourist attractions.

Routes from San Miguel → *For listings, see pages 63-66.*

Several routes radiate outwards from San Miguel. A paved road runs south to the Pacific Highway. Go south along it for 12 km, where a dirt road leads to Playa El Cuco (bus 320 from San Miguel, US$1.50). A mainly paved, reasonable road goes to west to San Jorge and Usulután: leave the Pan-American Highway 5 km west of San Miguel, where the road passes hills and coffee plantations with good views of the San Miguel volcano.

Another route heads northeast to the small town of Jocorro, where the road splits with options to Honduras. Heading north, San Francisco Gotera leads to the Perquín crossing; east of Jocorro the road leads to the border crossing at El Amatillo; and directly east from San Miguel lies La Unión, with connections north to El Amatillo.

San Miguel

Sleeping 🛏

China House **2**	El Mandarín **6**	Plaza Floresta **1**
Comfort Inn Real **4**	King Palace **3**	Trópico Inn **8**
	Motel Millián **5**	Victoria **10**

San Francisco Gotera and around

The capital of Morazán Department can be reached directly from the Oriente terminal in San Salvador, or from San Miguel (bus No 328). There are places to stay (see Sleeping, page 64).

Beyond San Francisco, the road runs to **Jocaitique** (there is a bus) from where an unpaved road climbs into the mountains through pine forests to **Sabanetas**, near the Honduran border. Accommodation is available at Jocaitique and Sabanetas.

Northeast of San Francisco is **Corinto** ① *20 mins north of the village on foot, just east of the path to the Cantón Coretito, open daily*, which has two rock overhangs showing faint evidence of pre-Columbian wall paintings. Take an early bus, No 327, from San Miguel, US$1.

Ciudad Segundo Montes and around

Eight kilometres north of San Francisco Gotera is Ciudad Segundo Montes, a group of villages housing 8500 repatriated Salvadorean refugees (the community is named after one of the six Jesuit priests murdered at the Central American University in November 1989). Schafic Vive is a small museum with information on the community. If you wish to visit contact **PRODETUR** ① *T2680-4086*, for information. No formal accommodation is available.

Fourteen kilometres north of San Francisco is **Delicias de la Concepción**, where fine decorated hammocks and ceramics are made. The prices are good and the people are helpful; worth a visit. Buses every 20 minutes from San Francisco.

Perquín and around → *Altitude: 1200 m. Population: 3158.*

Perquín – meaning 'Road of the Hot Coals'– is 205 km from San Salvador and was the guerrillas' 'capital', and the scene of much military activity. War damage used to be visible around the town, but all is now peaceful and the scenery is very beautiful, surrounded by pine-topped mountains. There is a small central square with a Casa de la Cultura, and post office. Opposite is the plain Iglesia Católica Universal Progresista, next to which is POLITUR, the very helpful and friendly police station. The police may give you a lift to the tourist office, below, now that it has rather inconveniently moved. It is now on the outskirts of town, past the turn-off to La Posada de Don Manuel, jointly run by **PRODETUR** and **Perkin Tours** travel agency ① *T2680-4311, www.rutadepazelsalvador.com, Mon-Fri 0800-1700*.

The **Museo de la Revolución** ① *T7942-3721, daily 0800-1700, US$1.20, no photos or filming allowed, guided tours in Spanish, camping permitted, US$1*, clearly signposted from the plaza, has temporary exhibits as well as one on Archbishop Romero and all the gory details of his murder – nothing is spared. The museum, run by ex-guerrillas, is badly lit, but fascinating with photographs, propaganda posters, explanations, objects, pictures of the missing, and military paraphernalia. In the garden is the wreckage of an American-made helicopter, shot down by guerrillas in 1984. Sprawled like a piece of modern art, it would look at home in a contemporary art gallery. There is also a room where a recreated cabin shows the place from where the clandestine radio *Venceremos* broadcast their programmes during the war.

Behind the town is the **Cerro de Perquín** ① *US$0.25 to climb, it is advisable to bring a guide*. The views are fantastic with the town below nestling in the tropical scenery, green parrots flying through the pine trees, and the mountains stretching towards the border with Honduras. The **Festival de Invierno**, 1-6 August, is a mixture of music, exhibitions and film. Book accommodation in advance if planning to come for the festival. The **Festival de San Sebastián** is on 21-22 January, and the celebration of the **Virgen del Tránsito**, the patron saint of the church, takes place 14-15 August.

Nearby villages such as Arambala and El Mozote can be visited, or you can take a walking tour. At El Mozote is a memorial to a massacre that took place in 1981, during which more than 800 people, among them children and babies, were brutally murdered. Five kilometres west of Perquín is **Arambala**, which is slowly being rebuilt. Locals will give you a tour (free, but tips appreciated) of the town and church, which has been largely rebuilt since being destroyed by fire in the 1980s; a sad and deeply moving experience, well worth the effort. Opposite the church is a small crafts shop run by a local women's cooperative, some of whom are also guides. Near Perquín, turn-off 2 km south, are the park and trails of **Cerro Pelón**. Nearby is **El Llano del Muerto**, a tourist area of naturally heated pools and wells. North of Perquín, straddling the border with Honduras, is one of the few unpolluted rivers in the country. The people of Morazán are more reserved with strangers than in the rest of El Salvador. If travelling on your own, 4WD is advised.

Ruta de Paz run by **Perkin Tours** ① *T2680-4086, perkintours@yahoo.es, daily 0800-1700, 0800-2100 during the winter festival*, provides walks, culture and adventure tourism, and can organize accommodation. Tours last for between 25 minutes and two days, and are for one to 10 people. Ask for Serafín Gómez, who is in charge of the tours.

Santa Rosa de Lima → *Population: 27,693.*
The shortest route from San Miguel to the Honduran border takes the Ruta Militar northeast through Santa Rosa de Lima to the Goascarán bridge at El Amatillo, a total of 58 km on paved road.

Santa Rosa is a charming little place with a wonderful colonial church set in the hillside. There are gold and silver mines, a market on Wednesday, and a curiously large number of pharmacies and shoe shops. The FMLN office has details about the **Codelum Project**, a refugee camp in Monte Barrios. The fiesta is on 22-31 August.

La Unión → *For listings, see pages 63-66. Population: 34,045.*

It is another 42 km from San Miguel to the port of La Unión (formerly known as Cutuco), on the Gulf of Fonseca. The spectacular setting on the west shore of the gulf does little to offset the heat and the faded glory of this port town which handles half the country's trade. Shortly before entering the town, the Pan-American Highway turns north for 33 km to the Goascarán bridge at **El Amatillo** on the border with Honduras. A project to inaugurate the modern port of La Unión is scheduled to happen in the near future. This huge project includes foreign investments, such as a large Spanish tuna fish processing plant, with supporting infrastructure including new roads, hotels and a school running training in logistics and tourism.

Around la Unión
Conchagua is worth visiting to see one of the few old colonial churches in the country, and there is a good bus service from La Unión (No 382, US$0.10). The church was begun in 1693, after the original Conchagua had been moved to its present site following repeated attacks on the island settlements by the English. There are fiestas on

18-21 January and 24 July. There is also **Volcán Conchagua** (1243 m) which can be climbed but is a hard walk, particularly near the top where protective clothing is useful against the vegetation. It's about four hours up and two hours down, but you will be rewarded with superb views over Volcán San Miguel to the west and the Gulf of Fonseca, which is bordered by El Salvador, Honduras and Nicaragua (where the Cosigüina volcano is prominent) to the east.

In the Gulf of Fonseca are the Salvadorean islands of **Isla Zacatillo**, **Isla Conchagüita** and the largest, **Isla Meanguera** (about 4 km by 7 km). English and Spanish pirates occupied Isla Meanguera in the late 1600s, and international claims remained until the International Court of Justice in The Hague awarded the island to El Salvador in 1992, in preference to claims from Honduras and Nicaragua.

A *lancha* leaves La Unión for the town of **Meanguera del Golfo**, on Meanguera. The journey across the gulf is beautiful – tranquil waters, fishing boats and views to the surrounding mountains. The island has secluded beaches with good bathing, for example Majahual (a 45-minute walk), fringed with palm trees. About 2400 people live on this carefree island, where painted boats float in the cove surrounded by small *tiendas* and *comedores* that serve fish, shark and prawns. The highest point on the island is **Cerro de Evaristo** at 512 m. Launches leave La Unión daily at 1000, or private boats may leave earlier when full; the journey takes 45 minutes. It's possible to arrange transport with a local boatman to Coyolito (Honduras), Isla Amapala, or for day trips around the gulf (about US$80), but make sure the price is agreed beforehand. You can travel to Honduras or Nicaragua if you have visited immigration in La Unión first to get the necessary paperwork.

Eastern El Salvador listings

For Sleeping and Eating price codes and other relevant information, see page 10.

◯ Sleeping

San Vicente *p58, map p58*
$ Central Park, on Parque Central, T2393-0383. Good, clean rooms, with bath, a/c and phone. Cheaper with fan, cheaper still without TV. Café and restaurant downstairs.
$ Estancia Familiar, El Calvario (corner in front of Pollo Campero), budget option in town.

San Miguel *p59, map p60*
Most hotels are on the entrance roads, although there are plenty of cheap places near the bus station.
$$$ Hotel Comfort Inn Real, Av Roosevelt, in front of Metrocentro, T2600-0202, www.choicehotels.com. Comfortable, businesslike hotel, spick and span if spartan

rooms, with a/c, cable TV; excellent buffet breakfast, tiny pool and adjacent bar/restaurant; laundromat. Convenient for Metrocentro mall, opposite.
$$ El Mandarín, Av Roosevelt Norte, T2669-6969. A/c, pool, good Chinese restaurant.
$$ Hotel Plaza Floresta, Av Roosevelt Sur 704, T2640-1549, www.hotelplazafloresta.com. Pleasant, clean rooms facing central courtyard with tiny swimming pool; cable TV, Wi-Fi access. Handy location for nearby restaurants and nightlife.
$$ Motel Millián, Panamericana Km 136, in front of the Military Hospital, T2683-8100. Pool and a good restaurant. Recommended, value for money.
$$ Trópico Inn, Av Roosevelt Sur 303, T2682-1082, tropicoinn@yahoo.com. Clean and comfortable, with reasonable restaurant, swimming pool, garden and safe parking for motorbikes. Recommended.

$$ Victoria, 8a Av Sur 101, El Calvario
T2660-7208, hotelvictoriasanmiguel2008@
hotmail.com. Private bath with a/c
and cable TV.

$ China House, 15 Av Norte, Pan-americana
Km 137.5, T2669-5029. Clean, friendly.

$ King Palace, opposite the bus station.
Good breakfast.

San Francisco Gotera *p61*
$$-$ Hospedaje San Francisco,
Av Morazán 29, T2654-0066. Nice garden
and hammocks.

Perquín and around *p61*
$$ Arizona T2634-8990, at entrance to town
on main street towards El Llano del Muerto.

$$ Hotel Perkin Lenca, Km 205.5 Carretera
a Perquín, T2680-4080, www.perkinlenca.
com. Cosy Swiss cabins with piping hot
showers and thick blankets. Excellent meals
in restaurant **La Cocina de Ma'Anita**, with
panoramic terrace overlooking forested hills,
open daily 0700-1900. US owner Ronald
organizes tours to El Mozote with former
guerrilla guides, a bit grim but very moving.

$$ Las Margaritas, T2613-1930, at the
entrance to Perquín village.

$ Cocina Mama Toya y Mama Juana, at
the entrance of Perquin village, T2680-4045.
Small rooms with 3 beds, shared bath, parking.

$ La Posada de Don Manuel, 5 mins
from Perquín at the bottom of the hill,
CTE Perquín T2680-4037. Previously called
El Gigante, countless partitioned rooms
that would probably be noisy if full, but
rarely are. Clean, with cold showers and
meals. Have highly recommended restaurant
and organize tours with guides. Friendly.

Camping
It's possible to camp in the grounds of
the **Museo de la Revolución**, near a crater
formed by a 227-kg bomb dropped in
Aug 1981. Ask in the nearby *tiendas*.

Near the Río Zapo, **PRODETUR**, T2680-
4311, www.rutadepazelsalvador.com, has a
great campground with facilities, and there
are guides who can give you a tour of the
area. Good for both trekking and hiking.
There is also a simple cabin for rent here.

Santa Rosa de Lima *p62*
$ Florida, Ruta Militar, T2641-2020. Helpful,
fairly clean, basic, with 3 parking spaces
(arrive early).

$ Hospedaje Mundial, near the market.
Basic rooms with fan. Friendly, lots of parking.

$ Recreo, 2 blocks from town centre in front
of police station and Telecom, 4 Av Norte,
Barrio el Recreo, T2641-2126. Basic fan
rooms, noisy but friendly. Recommended.

La Unión *p62*
$ San Francisco, Calle General Menéndez
6-3, Barrio Concepción, T2604-4159. Clean
and friendly, some rooms with hammocks
and fan. Noisy and has some water supply
problems, but OK. Safe parking.

Around La Unión *p62*
$$$ Hotel Joya del Golfo, Isla de Meanguera,
T2648-0072. Wonderfully relaxing hotel in
the next bay beyond the harbour (ask the
lancha from La Unión to drop you off), run by
extremely hospitable US-Salvadorean family.
4 lovely rooms, beautifully furnished, with
4-poster beds, a/c, cable TV and balcony.
Excellent food in cosy family lounge, with
books, games and DVDs. Kayaks for guests
and boat to nearby beaches (US$10), plus
hikes around island. Reservations essential.
Highly recommended.

$ Hotel Paraíso, Meanguera del Golfo.
Has rooms with TV, private bath and hot
water. Recommended.

🍴 Eating

Ilobasco *p57*
There are 2 pizzerias, several local *comedores*,
a **Pollo Campero** and a **Taco Hut**.

$$ Restaurante Ricky, at 3 Av Sur.
The town's only real restaurant with
à la carte dining.

San Vicente *p58, map p58*

The San Vicente Gastronomical festival is
held on the last Sat of the month at the
central park. Close to Hotel Central Park are
Pops and **La Nevería**, for good ice cream.
$ Acapulco, by the central market. Good.
$ Casablanca, next to the park, T2393-0549.
Good shrimps, steaks, and you can swim
in their pool for US$1.15.
$ Comedor Rivoli, Av María de los Angeles
Miranda. Good breakfast and lunches. Clean.
$ Evergreen. Bar and restaurant. Wed-Sun.

San Miguel *p59, map p60*

Try *bocadillos de totopostes*, maize balls with
either chilli or cheese; and *tustacos*, which
are like small tortillas with sugar or honey.
Both are delicious and traditional.
$ El Gran Tejano, 4 Calle Pte, near the
cathedral. Great steaks.
$ Restaurant Perkin Lenca, Km 205.5
Carretera a Perquín, T2680-4080,
www.perkinlenca.com. Daily 0700-2000.
Part of the hotel of the same name, this
restaurant serves traditional food.

Perquín and around *p61*

$ Antojitos Marisol, T2680-4063, near
the church on the south side of the
plaza. Simple food and open late.
$ Comedor Blanquita, T2680-4223 near
the church in the centre, *comida a la vista*
and snacks.
$ La Cocina de Mi Abuela, at the entrance
to town. T2502-2630, popular with locals
with good, local dishes.

Santa Rosa de Lima *p62*

$$ Martina, near the bridge. Good food
including *sopa de apretadores* for US$7.
$ Chayito, Ruta Militar. Buffet, *comedor*.

La Unión *p62*

Bottled water is hard to find, but *agua helada*
from clean sources is sold (US$0.25 a bag).
There are several cheap *comedores* to choose
from, try **Comedores Gallego ($)** and **Rosita
($)**, recommended. **Comedor Tere ($)**, Av
General Menéndez 2.2, is also fairly good.
$$ Amanecer Marino, on the waterfront.
Beautiful view of the bay and good for
watching the world go by. Serves seafood.
$ Las Lunas, 3 blocks from the central park.
Nice atmosphere. Very popular among locals.
$ Restaurante Puerto Viejo, located in front
of El Dragón. Big portions, cheap. Best seafood
in town – try *tazón de sopa de pescado*.

⊖ Transport

Cojutepeque *p57*

Bus No113 from Oriente terminal in
San Salvador (US$0.80); buses leave
from Cojutepeque on the corner of the
plaza, 2 blocks from the main plaza.

San Sebastián *p58*

Bus No 110 from the Oriente terminal
runs from San Salvador to San Sebastián
(1½ hrs, US$1). There are also buses
from Cojutepeque.

San Vicente *p58, map p58*

Bus No116 from Oriente terminal, **San
Salvador**, every 10 mins or so (1½ hrs,
US$0.90). Returning to the capital, catch bus
from the bus station, Av Victoriano Rodríguez
y Juan Crisóstomo Segovia; outside the
cathedral; or on the road out of town.
To **Zacatecoluca**, No 177 (US$0.50) from
bus station. Buses to some local destinations
leave from the street that runs west to east
through the market. You have to take 2 buses
to get to **San Miguel** (see below), the first
to the Pan-American Hwy, where there is a
bus and food stop, then another on to San
Miguel (US$1.50 total).

San Miguel *p59, map p60*
Bus Nos 301, 306 and 346 from Oriente terminal, **San Salvador** US$2.50, every 30 mins from 0500 to 1630, 2½ hrs. There are also 3 comfortable express buses daily, 2 hrs, US$5.

There are frequent buses to the Honduran border at **El Amatillo**, US$1. 4 buses, No 332A, daily to **Perquín**, from 0600-1240, 2¾ hrs, US$1.60. Direct to Tegucigalpa, with King Quality Bus, T2271-0307, www.kingqualityca.com/, daily at 0830 and 1630, 6 hrs, US$35

Perquín and around *p61*
Bus From **San Miguel**, bus No 332A (2¾ hrs, US$1.50). The bus from Terminal Oriente in **San Salvador** (4½ hrs) is very crowded, luggage a hindrance. Bus or truck from **Cd Segundo Montes**. Transport back to Cd Segundo Montes or San Miguel may be difficult in the afternoons.

Car If you're driving fill your tank before getting to Perquín because the last petrol station is 20 mins from the city and closes at 1700.

Santa Rosa de Lima *p62*
Bus To the Honduran border every 15 mins, US$0.50. Direct buses also to **San Salvador**, No 306, from 0400 until 1400, US$3.25, 3½ hrs.

La Unión *p62*
Bus The terminal is at 3 Calle Pte (block 3). To **San Salvador**, bus 304, US$2, 2-3 hrs, many daily, direct or via San Miguel, 1 passes the harbour at 0300. Bus 324 to **San Miguel,** US$1. Bus to Honduran border at **El Amatillo**, No 353, US$1.80.

ⓘ Directory

San Vicente *p58, map p58*
Banks Banco Hipotecario on main plaza, exchange counter at side. Also branches of HSBC, **Citi Bank** and **Banco Agrícola Casa de Cambio León**, Calle Dr Antonio J Cañas, off northeast corner of main plaza. **Post** In Gobernación, 2 Av Norte y Calle 1 de Julio 1823. **Telephone** Telecom, 2 Av Norte/Av Canónigo Raimundo Lazo, southeast of plaza.

San Miguel *p59, map p60*
Banks Daily 0900-1600. **Citi Bank** will change TCs, but you must produce receipt of purchase. **Banco Agrícola** is next to Trópico Inn. **Casa de Cambio Lego**, 2 Calle Pte, overlooking market. **Police** Emergency T911.

La Unión *p62*
Banks Open daily 0900-1600. **Scotiabank, HSBC and Western Union** between bus terminal and harbour, have 24-hr ATMs. **Customs** 3 Av Norte 3.9. **Immigration** Av General Cabañas and 1 Av Norte. **Internet** Infocentro, 1 Calle Pte, 2-4 Av Norte, Mon-Fri. **Police** Opposite Immigration office.

Pacific coast

Running the length of the country to the south, the Pacific coastline is a blend of stunning views, quiet beaches and private resorts. If basking in the sun isn't enough, the coast is a big hit with the surf crowd as some of the best surfing spots are located in the departments of La Libertad and Las Flores in San Miguel. For a little more activity, you can go west and visit the impressive Parque Nacional El Imposible. Heading east towards Nicaragua, the islands of the Gulf of Fonseca are equally cut off.

La Libertad → *For listings, see pages 72-76. Population: 35,997.*

Just before Santa Tecla, a branch road turns south for 24 km to the small fishing port of La Libertad, 34 km from San Salvador and just 25 minutes from the Comalapa International Airport. This is a popular, laid-back seaside resort in the dry season but is not very clean. However, the whole area has been remodelled and now boasts an amphitheatre, soccer and basketball courts and a **Complejo Turístico** where the old naval building once stood, with a *malecón* and several restaurants. **Tourist office** ① *T2346-1634, Mon-Fri 0800-1600, Sat, Sun 0900-1300*. The pier is worth seeing for the fish market awnings and, when the fleet is in, for the boats hauled up out of the water along its length. The cemetery by the beach has tombstones painted in the national colours, blue and white. On the seafront are several hotels and restaurants. At a small plaza, by the **Punta Roca** restaurant, the road curves left to the point, offering fine views of La Libertad bay and along the coast. The market street is two blocks inland across from the central church. The coast to the east and west has good fishing, surfing and bathing. The beaches are black volcanic sand (which can get very hot).

La Libertad gets very crowded at weekends and holidays and for overnight stays the beaches to the west of La Libertad are better. Service can be off-hand. Dedicated surfers may wish to stay for a while, as the breaks at Punta Roca in Puerto La Libertad are rated among the best 10 in the world. The season runs from November to April and the surf is excellent. Watch your belongings on the beach and don't stay out alone late at night.

The town holds an annual **Gastronomic Festival** in early December and has resurrected the tradition of *lunadas* (full-moon parties) in the dry season. Bonfires are lit on the beach, restaurants stay open late offering *comida típica*, and some places provide live music and themed nights. Find local information in Spanish at www.puertolalibertad.com.

Around La Libertad

The **Costa del Bálsamo** (Balsam coast), running west from La Libertad and Acajutla, gives its name to the pain-relieving balsam, once a major export of the region. On the steep slopes of the departments of Sonsonate and La Libertad, scattered balsam trees are still tapped for their aromatic juices. Buses travel along the coast to Sonsonate (at 0600 and 1300) and the journey offers stunning views of the rugged volcanic coast. The municipalities of San Julián, Cuisnahuat, Ixhuatan, Tepecoyo, Talnique, Jayaque, Chiltuipan, Comasagua and Teotepeque are all situated along the balsam coast. On the road from San Salvador to La Libertad is **Plaza Turística Zaragoza** ① *Tue-Sun 1000-1900, where you will find handicrafts, restaurants and amenities for children.*

At the very entrance of Puerto La Libertad is the **El Faro** shopping center, with **Selectos** supermarket, a shoe shop, **Nevería** ice cream shop and fried chicken **Pollo Campero**.

The eastern end of La Libertad is **Playa La Paz or Punta Roca**, 2 km beyond which is **Playa Obispo**. About 1 km east of La Curva, on the right towards San Diego is the **Fisherman's Club** ① *T2262-4444, entry US$6*, with pool, tennis courts and a good restaurant. The beach is good too, but beware of the rip tide; it's only advisable for surfers.

West of La Libertad → *For listings, see pages 72-76.*

Continuing west from **Playa Conchalío** at Km 38 you reach **Playa El Majahual**, which does not have a safe reputation, nor is it very clean, but offers good waves for surfing. A little further on is **Playa El Cocal** and **Playa San Blas**. On both beaches there are several hotels catering primarily for surfers. One of the most popular beaches for foreigners is **Playa El Tunco**. To get here take bus No 80 from La Libertad and get off at the turn-off where all the surfer hotels signs are posted (**Roca Sunzal** is the most visible one). It is then a short walk (a couple of blocks) to the seafront. This is one of the best surfing beaches in this area with the two breaks, El Sunzal and La Bocana, both easily accessible. Club Salvadoreño ① www.clubsalvadoreno.com, and **Club Tecleño** both have their beach premises here and El Tunco itself has several hotels and restaurants.

Further up the road at Km 43.5 is **El Sunzal**. Although the breaks are amazing at Sunzal, the small hotels are not as safe as at El Tunco and there have been reports of theft on the beach at dusk, so choose to stay at El Tunco. The exception in El Sunzal is the luxury hotel **Casa de Mar**, which is located just in front of the breaks, and is an option if you want a splurge or to dine in their gourmet seafood restaurant, **Café Sunzal**, which has great food and panoramic views of the beach.

At Km 49.5 is **Playa Palmarcito**. This tiny and inviting beach is great for escaping the crowds and is good for novice surfers, as the breaks are not as violent as on other beaches. Located just in front of the beach is **Restaurante Las Palmas**, offering great meals and low prices. An option for a few night's stay is **Hotel El Palmarcito**, which also has a restaurant, surf board rental and classes. Perched atop a cliff next to Palmarcito is the **Atami Beach Club** ① *T2223-9000, access for US and other non-Central American passport-holders is US$10, including a cabaña for changing*, a beautiful place with a large pool, private beach, expensive restaurant, two bars and gardens. At the turn-off to the beach along the highway (next to police station) is the **Hotel Bosques del Río** (same owner as **Restaurante Las Palmeras**), where you can ask for discounts for longer stays.

Just a couple of kilometres out of La Libertad on the Carretera Litoral is **Parque Nacional Walter Deininger** ① *run by the Ministry of Tourism, T2243-7835, www.el salvador.travel, for more information contact ISTU on T2222-8000, www.istu.gob.sv*, simply present your passport at the gate. There are rivers and caves, and the park is great for hiking. There is even a seed bank for endangered tree species, an array of medicinal plants and a nursery. The views are fantastic and it's a good way to learn more about the flora and fauna, guides are available upon request.

At Km 53.5 is **Playa El Zonte**, is another favourite among foreign tourists. It's a bit safer and quieter than El Tunco, being further away from La Libertad. The top-notch surf breaks has made El Zonte a place people stay longer than anticipated, and there are several well-established hotels with restaurant service. There are also several informal, cheap cafés and room rentals down at the beach.

The Carretera Litoral continues for a further 40 km or so to Acajutla past rocky bays, remote black-sand beaches and through tunnels. Take great care if you bathe along this coast, as it can be dangerous.

Acajutla and around → *Population: 52,359.*

At the junction of San Julián, a short journey south from Sonsonate, the coastal road heads south to the lowland city of Acajutla, El Salvador's main port serving the western and central areas, 85 km from San Salvador (the port is 8 km south of the Coastal Highway). It is a popular seaside resort during the summer for Salvadoreans, but lodging in the village is not considered safe for foreigners. There are some good seafood restaurants with panoramic views.

The rocky beach of **Los Cóbanos** (14 km south of Acajutla via San Julián, bus from Sonsonate) is very popular with weekending Salvadoreans and has one of only two coral reefs along the entire Central American Pacific coast, making it a popular dive spot. Fishermen arrange boat trips; negotiate a price. José Roberto Suárez at **Los Cobanos Village Lodge** ① *T2420-5248, sas_tun@hotmail.com*, speaks English and can be of assistance when renting boats and diving equipment.

The paved coastal road heads west running along the coast for 43 km before reaching the Guatemalan frontier at **La Hachadura**.

The black-sand beaches northwest of Acajutla at **Metalío** and Costa Azul (mostly full of private beach houses) and **Barra de Santiago** are recommended, although there are few public facilities. Barra de Santiago is a peninsula, 30 km west of Acajutla, the beach is reached along a 7 km compact dirt road or across a beautiful lagoon. The entire area is a protected natural area is in the process of being declared an ecological reserve to protect endangered species, including turtles, crocodiles and sea falcons. The *garza azul* (blue heron) is one of the amazing rare birds only found here. The mangrove is the third largest in El Salvador. This beach has an island named **El Cajete,** which has an archaeological site dating back to around AD 900. There are several pyramids but the area has not been excavated. El Capricho Beach House ① *T2260-2481*, has a beautiful beach-front hotel here (see Sleeping, page 73; same owners as **Ximena's** in San Salvador, see page 25).

Parque Nacional El Imposible

① *Park entrance is US$6, payable at the gate. For more information contact Salvanatura office, 33 Av Sur 640, Col Flor Blanca, San Salvador, T2279-1515, www.salvanatura.org. Voluntary donation of US$4-5 a day. To get to the park, take the San Salvador–Sonsonate bus, and then bus No 259 to Cara Sucia. Pickups leave for the park at 1100 and 1400. From Guatemala and the border, regular buses heading for San Salvador pass through Cara Sucia from where you catch the 1100 and 1400 pickups.*

So called because of the difficulty of transporting coffee through its ravines and down to the coast, today this 'impossibility' has helped preserve some of the last vestiges of El Salvador's flora and fauna on the rocky slopes and forests of the coastal **Cordillera de Apaneca**. Mule trains used to travel through the region, navigating the steep passes from which the park takes its name.

Among the mammals are puma, ocelot, agouti and ant bear; the birds include black-crested eagle, white hawk and other birds of prey, black and white owls, and woodpeckers. There is also a wide variety of reptiles, amphibians and insects, the greatest diversity in the country. There are eight different strata of forest, and over 300 species of tree have been identified. There is a small visitor centre, and rivers and natural pools to swim in. Trained naturalist guides from the nearby community of San Miguelito accompany visitors into the park, helping to identify season specific trails and routes, and pointing out interesting plants, animals and other attractions along the way.

East of La Libertad → *For listings, see pages 72-76.*

The second route to La Unión runs east through the southern cotton lands. It begins on a four-lane motorway to the airport at Comalapa. The first place of any importance is at Km 13, **Santo Tomás** where there are pre-Hispanic ruins at **Cushululitán**, a short distance north. A road to the east, rising to 1000 m, runs south of Lago de Ilopango to join the Pan-American Highway beyond Cojutepeque. From Santo Tomás it's 10 km on to **Olocuilta**, an old town famed for its church and known worldwide for its rice dough *pupusas*. It hosts a colourful market on Sundays under a great tree. Both Santo Tomás and Olocuilta can be reached by bus 133 from San Salvador. The highway to the airport crosses the Carretera Litoral (CA 2) near the towns of San Luis Talpa and Comalapa. The coastal road goes east, through Rosario de la Paz, across Río Jiboa and on to Zacatecoluca.

Costa del Sol

Just after Rosario, a branch road to the south leads to **La Herradura** (bus 153 from Terminal del Sur to La Herradura, US$1.25, 1½ hours) and the Playa Costa del Sol on the Pacific, which is being developed as a tourist resort. The beach is on a narrow peninsula, the length of which are private houses which prevent access to the sand until you reach the **Turicentro** ① *0800-1800*. Here, *cabañas* can be rented for the day or for 24 hours, but they are not suitable for sleeping. Playa Costa del Sol is crowded at weekends and holidays, as there are extensive sandy beaches. However, the sea has a mild undertow; so go carefully until you are sure. Expensive hotels are continuously popping up but prices are a bit over the top; budget travellers might choose some of the smaller hotels by Playa Los Blancos. On the road to Costa del Sol, there is also a great water park, **Atlantis Water Park** ① *Km 51, carretera Costa del Sol, T2211-4103, www.atlantis.com.sv, US$8*. It's on bus routes No 495 and 143 (every 15 minutes). Options from San Salvador, include hotel pickup, small lunch and entrance from US$15-20.

Isla Tasajera

At the southeast end of the Costa del Sol road, near the **Pacific Paradise** hotel, a ferry (US$1.75) leaves for Isla Tasajera in the Estero de Jaltepeque (tidal lagoon). For boat excursions, take the Costa del Sol bus to the last stop at La Puntilla and negotiate with the local boatmen. Boat hire for the day costs US$75, including pilot. It's a great trip into the lagoon, with mangroves, dolphin watching and trips up to the mouth of the Río Lempa (the longest river in the country).

Zacatecoluca → *Altitude: 201 m. Population: 65,826.*
The capital of La Paz Department is 56 km from San Salvador by road and 19 km south of San Vicente. This is a good place to buy hammocks (for example nylon 'doubles', US$13). José Simeón Cañas, who abolished slavery in Central America, was born here. There is a cathedral in the Moorish style and an excellent art gallery as well as a mall with a supermarket and several stores.

Ichanmichen
ⓘ *Admission and car parking US$0.75 per person, bungalow rental US$4.*
Near the town is the park and Turicentro of Ichanmichen ('the place of the little fish'). It is crossed by canals and decorated with natural spring pools where you can swim. It is very hot but there is plenty of shade.

Usulután, Playa El Espino and Laguna El Jocotal
About 110 km from the capital is Usulután, capital of its department. It's a large, dirty and unsafe place, and only useful as a transit point (bus 302 from San Salvador, US$1.40). The coastal highway goes direct from Usulután to La Unión.

Playa El Espino can be reached from Usulután, by car (4WD), pickup or slow bus; it is very remote but lovely. Some small hotels and restaurants operate, but most only at weekends. To visit the reserve, enquire at the entrance; hire a boat to see more.

Beyond Usulután, the impressive silhouette of **Volcán Chaparrasque** rises out of the flat coastal plain. Two roads go northeast to San Miguel, the first from 10 km along at El Tránsito, the second a further 5 km east, which keeps to the low ground south and east of Volcán San Miguel. Two kilometres beyond this turning on the Carretera Litoral is a short road to the right leading to Laguna El Jocotal, a national nature reserve supported by the World Wildlife Fund, which has an abundance of birds and snakes.

Playa El Cuco and around
ⓘ *Bus No 320 to San Miguel, US$0.45, 1 hr, last bus 1600.*
About 12 km from the junction for San Miguel there is a turning to the right leading in 7 km to Playa El Cuco, a popular beach with several cheap places to stay near the bus station. The main beach is liable to get crowded and dirty at weekends and holidays, but is deserted mid-week. Single women should take care here; locals warn against walking along the beach after sunset. Cases of malaria have been reported. Another popular beach, **El Tamarindo**, is reached by following the coastal road a little further before taking a right turn.

Pacific coast listings

For Sleeping and Eating price codes and other relevant information, see page 10.

😊 Sleeping

La Libertad *p67*
$$ Pacific Sunrise, Calle Obispo, entrance of La Libertad, T2346-2000, www.hotelesel salvador.com. Hotel with pool, restaurant and rooms overlooking the Obispo beach, which can be accessed via an ingenious pedestrian overpass. Best hotel in La Libertad and good rates if more people share the rooms.
$$ Rick, behind **Punta Roca**. Clean rooms with bath. Friendly, good value. Has a restaurant.
$ Comedor Margoth. Run-down but clean.
$ Hotel Surf Club, 2 Calle Pte 22-9. Big rooms, a/c, kitchen area. Supermarket downstairs.

West of La Libertad *p68*
Playa El Conchalío
$$ El Malecón de Don Lito, T2355-3201. Good for children, plenty of space.
$$ Los Arcos del Mediterráneo, T2335-3490, www.hotelmedplaz.com.sv. 300 m from beach. A/c, TV, safe and quiet, with pool, garden and restaurant.

Playa El Majahual
$$ Hotel El Pacífico, T2310-6504. Pool, restaurant.
$ Hotel y Restaurante Santa Fe, at the entrance to the Majahual beach, T2310-6508. Safe and nice, with pool. Recommended, relaxing and safe.

Playa El Cocal
$$ Punta Roca Surf Resort, T2300-0474, www.puntaroca.com.sv. Owned by National Champion Jimmy Rotherham, Punta Roca is an option for surfers (the beach has rocks!).

Playa El Sunzal
$ El Hostal at the entrance of Playa El Sunzal run by a couple of guys from the US.
$ Roots Camping, Km 42, Carretera Litoral, next to **Restaurante Roca Sunzal**, fruboza@ hotmail.com. Campsite with thatched-roof terrace for tents and hammocks.

Playa San Blas and Playa El Tunco
$$ Hotel Mopelia, T2389-6265, www.hotel mopelia-salvador.com. Owned by Frenchman Gilles, is a popular spot, also for its bar (open all week) and new pizzeria **Tunco Veloz**.
$$ Roca Sunzal, Km 42, T2389-6126, www.rocasunzal.com. Best hotel in El Tunco, beautifully located in front of the beach. Great views, pool, good food in restaurant. Value for money. They now have new suites with artsy and original decor. Good service. Recommended.
$ Casa Tamanique, a couple of blocks up the road from El Tubo, fernandosgallegos@ yahoo.com. Newcomer with a tiny hostel.
$ La Guitarra, www.surfingeltunco.com, T2389-6390. 18 rooms with and without a/c, discounts for longer stays, Wi-Fi.
$ La Sombra, info@lasombradelarte.com. Rooms with a/c and fan.
$ Papayas Lodge, T2389-6231, www.papayalodge.com. Family-run surf hostel. Clean rooms with fans, use of kitchen and safe. Owned by Salvadorean surf legend, Papaya. Board sales and repair and surf classes. Recommended.
$ Sol Bohemio, T7887-6241, www.sol bohemio.com. Reasonable rates, as do a couple of the smaller hostels, such as **Barriles**.

Playa Palmarcito
$$ Atami Beach Club, Km 49.5, T2335-7301, www.atami.com.sv. Good rooms. Swimming pool and water slide. Seafood restaurant. In the grounds of the club is a private *rancho*.

$ El Palmarcito, T7942-4879, www.elpalmarcito.com, surf lessons, board rental, restaurant, beachfront.

Playa El Zonte
$ Esencia Nativa, T7737-8879, www.esencianativa.com. Run by surfer Alex Novoa, with cheap rooms, dorm and pool. Popular restaurant serves range of options, including great veggie food and is busy at weekends. Surfing lessons and board rentals available. Popular with surfers.

$ Horizonte Surf Camp, T2323-0099, saburosurfcamp@hotmail.com. Simple bungalows, some with a/c, nice garden, pool, restaurant, board rental, clean, good service. Good choice for surfers. Beachfront restaurant offers good food. Room for up to 6 people on the 3rd floor. Great view.

$ La Casa de Frida Hotel, T2302-6068, www.lacasadefrida.com. Lodging in cabins behind restaurant with beachfront garden. Cosy place with hammocks.

Acajutla and around *p69*
$$$$ La Cocotera Resort & Ecolodge, Barra de Santiago, T2245-3691, www.lacocoteraresort.com. Rates per person are fully inclusive – full-board and airport transfers. Small luxurious resort with thatched bungalows on the beach and with mangroves behind; swimming pool, kayaks, and tours available. Very peaceful. Recommended.

$$ Los Cóbanos Village Lodge, Carretera Acajutla, turn right at **Restaurant Marsolie**, T2420-5248, www.loscobanos.com.sv. Beachfront cabins with pool and restaurant. Scuba-diving, surfing, fishing on offer. TV and internet available.

$$-$ Capricho Beach House, Barra de Santiago (same owners as **Ximena's**, see page 25), contact T2260-2481, www.ximenasguesthouse.com (under: Capricho). Private rooms with bath and

a/c, cabin with dorms and ceiling fan, clean and safe. Beautiful beach and located in a wildlife reserve, close to mangroves and the tip of the peninsula. Tours of the mangroves, fishing, surf lessons and board rental all available. Transport from the capital and tours to **Parque Nacional El Imposible** available. Recommended. Take direct bus No 285 to La Barra de Santiago, which departs twice daily from Sonsonate, or bus towards border and pickup from turn-off.

Parque Nacional El Imposible *p69*
$$ Hostal El Imposible, T2411-5484. With restaurant/bar area, swimming pool and small trail. 5 cabins sleeping 2-6 people have private bath, hot water and small terrace, also restaurant service. Information from **Salvanatura** in San Salvador, T2279-1515. www.salvanatura.org.

Costa del Sol *p70*
Cheaper accommodation can be found 1 km east at Playa Los Blancos and in La Herradura.
$$ Izalco Cabaña Club, T2338-2006. 30 rooms and a pool. Good value, seafood is a speciality.

$ Miny Hotel y Restaurant Mila, Km 66, opposite police station. Very friendly, owner Marcos speaks English. Clean, simple, fan, pool, good food, beach access. Take bus No 495 from Terminal Sur, San Salvador; buses are very crowded at weekends, but the resort is quiet during the week.

Playa El Cuco and around *p71*
$$ Trópico Club, 2.5 km along the coast from Playa El Cuco, T2682-1073, tropicoinn@yahoo.com. Several cabins, pool and open-air dining. Leads directly to the beach. Run by the **Trópico Inn** in San Miguel (T2661-1800) see page 63.

$ Cucolindo, 1 km along the coast, T2619-9012, hotelcucolindo@hotmail.com. Basic cabin for 4, with cold water. Mosquitos.

$ Los Leones Marinos, El Cuco, T2619-9015. Clean and tidy with bath.

Playa Las Flores
$$$$-$$$ Las Flores Surf Resort, close to Playa El Cuco, T2619-9118, www.lasflores resort.com. Run by surf expert Rodrigo Barraza, boutique hotel, catering mostly for foreign tourists making an excellent choice for an upscale budget.

Playa Torola
$$ Torola Cabaña Club, Km 175, T2681-5528. Pool looking out to sea, great open-air bar/restaurant, friendly. Welcoming owner, recommended.

Playa El Tamarindo
$$ Tropi Tamarindo, T2682-1073, www.tropicoinn.com.sv. Run by the **Trópico Inn** in San Miguel (T2661-1800), see page 63.

🍴 Eating

La Libertad *p67*
There are cheap restaurants near the pier, in the market, and around Playa La Paz, Playa El Obispo and El Sunzal. An area with new buildings located where the old Marina used to be close to the pier now hosts a series of great seafood eateries.
$$ El Nuevo Altamar, 4 Calle Pte, Playa La Paz, T2335-3235. Good for seafood, steaks and bird.
$$ Mariscos Freddy and **La Marea**, on the beach at Playa Obispo. Good-value seafood restaurants.
$$-$ Punta Roca, 5 Av Sur, T2335-3261. Mon-Fri 0800-2000, Sat and Sun 0800-2300. Try the shrimp soup. Owned by American ex-pat Robert Rotherham, father of the national surf champion Jimmy Rotherham.

Around La Libertad *p67*
East of the El Faro mall at the entrance there is a strip with very good restaurants. 2 of the best are:
$$ La Curva de Don Gere, T2335-34360. Legendary place run by Geremias Alvarado with several outlets in El Salvador (and the US). One of the trademarks is their seafood cream chowder in huge sizes including king crab legs and other goodies.
$$ La Dolce Vita, Playa Las Flores, 200 m east of the Shell gas station, T2335-3592. Excellent seafood and pasta restaurant.

West of La Libertad *p68*
El Sunzal
Around the Sunzal area are several very good restaurants, such **Hola Beto's**, **Las Pamas Mirador** and **La Curva de Don Gere**. All have beautiful vistas along the coast.
$$ Café Sunzal, Km 43.5 Carretera, T2389-6019, www.cafesunzal.com. Great seafood and steak house, exquisite international cuisine. Excellent views over El Sunzal beach.

Playa San Blas and Playa El Tunco
Tunco is on the rise and new places keep popping up.
$$ Hotel and Restaurante Roca Sunzal. Delicious seafood and a very good bar. All with an excellent beachfront location. Recommended.
$$ Hotel Mopelia (see Sleeping) has a pizzeria and their well-stocked bar is open all week.
$$-$ La Bocana, in front of the Tunco (pig). Owned and operated by Luis who's very friendly. Beachfront, offering great view from 2nd storey. Good seafood, great value.
$ Dale Dale Café, behind **Roca Sunzal**. Coffee shop serving delicious brownies, muffins and coffee to go with it.
$ Erika, T2389-6054. Run by owner Amelia Hernández. Very popular with the locals. 2nd-storey palm hatch with great atmosphere.

Playa El Zonte

$ Esencia Nativa (see Sleeping). Run by charismatic Alex Novoa, **Esencia Nativa** has an innovative menu, including good veggie options and pizzas, served at the poolside. Folks in the know come down from the capital just to get a bite.

$ Horizonte Surf Resort. A nice restaurant at the beachfront run by Japanese Saburo. The view from 2nd floor is especially lovely. Good value.

$ La Casa de Frida, El Zonte, T2253-2949, www.lacasadefrida.com. A great restaurant located in a large beachfront garden dotted with tables and hammocks.

Costa del Sol *p70*

$ Restaurante Kenny Mar, Km 60, Carretera Costa del Sol, Playa San Marcelino, T2338-2578. Delicious seafood with beachfront view.

▲ Activities and tours

La Libertad *p67*
Watersports

Look for board rentals and surf lessons at hostels on the coast west of Puerto La Libertad. Also look at www.sunzal.com, which offers great surfing tours combined with photography by local photographer, El Vaquero.

Punta Roca, restaurant in La Libertad, T2335-3261 www.puntarocarockets.com. Owner Robert Rotherham (father of Surf Champion Jimmy Rotherham) runs surfboard rental, including boards for both pros and beginners (see website for details). He also arranges excursions including deep-sea fishing for up to 3 people, see www.puntaroca.com.sv (which features webcam of area, surf and weather report) for more information. English spoken. Recommended.

⊖ Transport

La Libertad *p67*

Bus The station for the buses going down to Puerto La Libertad is now located at the 17th Av Sur at the intersection of Blv Venezuela by the general cemetery in San Salvador. The buses going to San Salvador from Puerto La Libertad leave from the terminal at the entrance of the city centre by the ball courts. Departures from Puerto La Libertad along the coast to Sonsonate at 0600.

For beaches around Acajutla and west, take the direct bus from Terminal de Occidente to Sonsonate and then on: No 285 to **Barra de Santiago**, No 28 to **Cara Sucia** and the border and No 252 to **Acajutla**.

For **Costa del Sol**, **Zacatecoluca** and connections toward eastern beaches go from Terminal del Sur by San Marcos in San Salvador.

Acajutla and around *p69*

Bus No 207 from Terminal Occidente, **San Salvador** (US$2.80), or No 252 from **Sonsonate** (US$0.30). 58 km from **Santa Ana**.

Zacatecoluca *p71*

Bus No133 from Terminal Sur, **San Salvador**. Direct bus to **La Libertad** 1540 (US$0.85), or take San Salvador bus, change at Comalapa, 2 hrs.

Playa El Cuco and around *p71*

Boat Boat from El Tamarindo across the bay leads to a short cut to **La Unión**.

Bus From **La Unión**, 20 mins.

La Libertad *p67*

Banks There are no credit card facilities or international ATMs in La Libertad. **Banco de Fomento Agropecuario**, Mon-Fri 0800-1600, Sat 0800-1200. Also has **Western Union**. **HSBC**, takes TCs. **Internet** Infocentros, in main street close to Puerto Bello, cheap. **Language school** 5 Av Norte, close to Punta Roca restaurant, T2449-0331, salvaspanischool@ mailcity.com. **Police** Calle Gerardo Barrios and 1 Av Sur. **Tourism police,** based here and patrol the town and beach areas at weekends. A tourist kiosk is in the new, gleaming white complex opposite the fish market pier, Mon-Fri 0800-1600, Sat and Sun 0900-1300, T2346-1634. **Post** Up the side of the Telecom office, 0800-1200, 1400-1700. **Telephone** Telepunto, next to Hotel Puerto Bello, 2 Calle Pte (0630-0830). Cheap rates. **Telecom** on same road.

Contents

Background

Regional history

Arrival of the American people

While controversy continues to surround the precise date humans arrived in the Americas, the current prevailing view suggests the first wave of emigrants travelled between Siberia and Alaska across the Bering Strait ice bridge created in the last Ice Age, approximately 15,000 years ago. Small hunter-gatherer groups quickly moved through the region, and in fertile lands they developed agriculture and settled. By 1500 BC sedentary villages were widespread in many parts of the Americas, including Central America, where stone-built cities and complex civilizations also began to emerge.

Pre-Columbian civilizations

Despite the wide variety of climates and terrains that fall within Central America's boundaries, the so-called Mesoamerican civilizations were interdependent, sharing the same agriculture based on maize, beans and squash, as well as many sociological traits. These included an enormous pantheon of gods, pyramid-building, a trade in valuable objects, hieroglyphic writing, astronomy, mathematics and a complex calendar system. Historians divide Mesoamerican civilizations into three broad periods, the **pre-Classic**, which lasted until about AD 300, the **Classic**, until AD 900, and the **post-Classic**, from AD 900 until the Spanish conquest.

Olmecs

Who precisely the Olmecs were, where they came from and why they disappeared is a matter of debate. It is known that they flourished from about 1400-400 BC, lived in the **Mexican Gulf coast** region between Veracruz and Tabasco, and that all later civilizations have their roots in Olmec culture. They are particularly renowned for their carved **colossal heads**, jade figures and altar. They gave great importance to the jaguar and the serpent in their imagery and built large ceremonial centres such as **San Lorenzo** and **La Venta**. The progression from the Olmec to the Maya civilization seems to have taken place at Izapa on the Pacific border of present-day Mexico and Guatemala.

Maya

The best known of the pre-Conquest civilizations were the Maya, thought to have evolved in a formative period in the **Pacific highlands** of Guatemala and El Salvador between 1500 BC and about AD 100. After 200 years of growth it entered what is known today as its Classic period, when the civilization flourished in Guatemala, El Salvador, Belize, Honduras and southern Mexico. The height of the Classic period lasted until AD 900, after which the Maya resettled in the Yucatán, possibly after a devastating famine, drought or peasant uprising. They then came under the influence of the central Mexican Toltecs, who were highly militaristic, until the Spanish conquest in the 16th century.

Throughout its evolution, Mayan civilization was based on independent city states that were governed by a theocratic elite of priests, nobles and warriors. Recent research has revealed that these cities, far from being the peaceful ceremonial centres once imagined, were **warring adversaries** striving to capture victims for sacrifice. This change in perception of the Maya was largely due to a greater understanding of Mayan **hieroglyphic writing**, which appears both on paper codices and on stone monuments. Aside from a gory preoccupation with sacrifice, Mayan culture was rich in **ceremony, art, science, folklore** and **dance**. Their cities were all meticulously designed according to strict and highly symbolic geometric rules: columns, figures, faces, animals, friezes, stairways and temples often expressed a date, a time or a specific astronomical relationship. Impressively, the Mayan calendar was so advanced that it was a nearer approximation to sidereal time than either the Julian or the Gregorian calendars of Europe; it was only .000069 of a day out of true in a year. The Maya also formulated the concept of 'zero' centuries in advance of the Old World, plotted the movements of the sun, moon, Venus and other planets, and conceived a time cycle of more than 1800 million days.

Conquest

It was only during his fourth voyage, in 1502, that **Columbus** reached the mainland of Central America. He landed in **Costa Rica** and Panama, which he called **Veragua**, and founded the town of Santa María de Belén. In 1508 Alonso de Ojeda received a grant of land on the Pearl coast east of Panama, and in 1509 he founded the town of San Sebastián, later moved to a new site called Santa María la Antigua del Darién (now in Colombia). In 1513 the governor of the colony at Darién was **Vasco Núñez de Balboa**. Taking 190 men he crossed the isthmus in 18 days and caught the first glimpse of the Pacific; he claimed it and all neighbouring lands in the name of the King of Spain. But from the following year, when **Pedrarias de Avila** replaced him as Governor, Núñez de Balboa fell on evil days, and he was executed by Pedrarias in 1519. That same year Pedrarias crossed the isthmus and founded the town of Panamá on the Pacific side. It was in April 1519, too, that **Cortés** began his conquest of Mexico. Central America was explored from these two nodal points of Panama and Mexico.

Settlement

The groups of Spanish settlers were few and widely scattered, a fundamental point in explaining the **political fragmentation** of Central America today. Panama was ruled from Bogotá, but the rest of Central America was subordinate to the Viceroyalty at Mexico City, with Antigua, Guatemala, as an Audiencia for the area until 1773, and thereafter Guatemala City. Panama was of paramount importance for colonial Spanish America for its strategic position, and for the trade passing across the isthmus to and from the southern colonies. The other provinces were of comparatively little value.

The small number of **Spaniards intermarried** freely with the locals, accounting for the predominance of mestizos in present-day Central America. But the picture has regional variations. In Guatemala, where there was the highest native population density, intermarriage affected fewer of the natives, and over half the population today is still purely *indígena* (**indigenous**). On the Meseta Central of Costa Rica, the natives were all but wiped out by disease and, as a consequence of this great disaster, there is a community of over two million whites, with little *indígena* admixture. **Blacks** predominate along the Caribbean coast of Central America. Most were brought in as cheap labour to work as railway builders and banana planters in the 19th century and canal cutters in the 20th. The **Garífuna** people, living between southern Belize and Nicaragua, arrived in the area as free people after African slaves and indigenous Caribbean people intermingled following a shipwreck off St Vincent.

Independence and after

On 5 November 1811, José **Matías Delgado**, a priest and jurist born in San Salvador, organized a revolt with another priest, Manuel José Arce. They proclaimed the Independence of El Salvador, but the Audiencia at Guatemala City suppressed the revolt and took Delgado prisoner. Eleven years later, in 1820, the revolution of Spain itself precipitated the Independence of Central America. On 24 February 1821, the Mexican **General Agustín de Iturbide** announced his **Plan de Iguala** for an independent Mexico. Several months later, the Central American *criollos* followed his example and announced their own **Declaration of Independence** in Guatemala City on 15 September 1821. Iturbide invited the provinces of Central America to join with him and, on 5 January 1822, Central America was annexed to Mexico. Delgado, however, refused to accept this decree and Iturbide, who had now assumed the title of **Emperor Agustín I**, sent an army south under Vicente Filísola to enforce it. Filísola had completed his task when he heard of Iturbide's abdication, and at once convened a general congress of the Central American provinces. It met on 24 June 1823, and thereafter established the **Provincias Unidas del Centro de América**. The Mexican Republic acknowledged their Independence on 1 August 1824, and Filísola's soldiers were withdrawn.

The United Provinces of Central America

In 1824, the first congress, presided over by Delgado, appointed a provisional governing *junta* which promulgated a constitution modelled on that of the United States. The Province of Chiapas was not included in the Federation, as it had already adhered to Mexico in 1821. Guatemala City, by force of tradition, soon became the seat of government.

The first president under the new constitution was **Manuel José Arce**, a liberal. One of his first acts was to abolish slavery. El Salvador, protesting that he had exceeded his powers, rose in December 1826. Honduras, Nicaragua and Costa Rica joined the revolt, and in 1828 **General Francisco Morazán**, in charge of the army of Honduras, defeated the federal forces, entered San Salvador and marched against Guatemala City. He captured the city on 13 April 1829, and established that contradiction in terms: a liberal dictatorship. Many conservative leaders were expelled and church and monastic properties confiscated. Morazán himself became President of the Federation in 1830. He was a man of considerable ability; he ruled with a strong hand, encouraged education, fostered trade and industry, opened the country to immigrants, and reorganized the administration. In 1835 the capital was moved to San Salvador.

These reforms antagonized the conservatives and there were several uprisings. The most serious revolt was among the *indígenas* of Guatemala, led by Rafael Carrera, an illiterate mestizo conservative and a born leader. Years of continuous warfare followed, during the course of which the Federation withered away. As a result, the federal congress passed an act which allowed each province to assume the government it chose, but the idea of a federation was not quite dead. Morazán became President of El Salvador. Carrera, who was by then in control of Guatemala, defeated Morazán in battle and forced him to leave the country. But in 1842, Morazán overthrew Braulio Carrillo, then dictator of Costa Rica, and became president himself. At once he set about rebuilding the Federation, but a popular uprising soon led to his capture. He was shot on 15 September 1842 and with him perished any practical hope of Central American political union.

The separate states
The history of **Guatemala**, **El Salvador**, **Honduras** and **Nicaragua** since the breakdown of federation has been tempestuous in the extreme (**Costa Rica**, with its mainly white population and limited economic value at the time, is a country apart, and **Panama** was Colombian territory until 1903). In each, the ruling class was divided into pro-clerical conservatives and anti-clerical liberals, with constant changes of power. Each was weak, and tried repeatedly to buttress its weakness by alliances with others, which invariably broke up because one of the allies sought a position of mastery. The wars were mainly ideological wars between conservatives and liberals, or wars motivated by inflamed nationalism. Nicaragua was riven internally by the mutual hatreds of the Conservatives of Granada and the Liberals of León, and there were repeated conflicts between the Caribbean and interior parts of Honduras. Despite the permutations and combinations of external and civil war there has been a recurrent desire to re-establish some form of **La Gran Patria Centroamericana**. Throughout the 19th century, and far into the 20th, there have been ambitious projects for political federation, usually involving El Salvador, Honduras and Nicaragua; none of them lasted more than a few years.

Regional integration
Poverty, the fate of the great majority, has brought about closer economic cooperation between the five republics, and in 1960 they established the **Central American Common Market** (CACM). Surprisingly, the Common Market appeared to be a great success until 1968, when integration fostered national antagonisms, and there was a growing conviction in Honduras and Nicaragua, which were doing least well out of integration, that they were being exploited by the others. In 1969 the 'Football War' broke out between El Salvador and Honduras, basically because of a dispute about illicit emigration by Salvadoreans into Honduras, and relations between the two were not normalized until 1980. Hopes for improvement were revived in 1987 when the Central American Peace Plan, drawn up by President Oscar Arias Sánchez of Costa Rica, was signed by the presidents of Guatemala, El Salvador, Honduras, Nicaragua and Costa Rica. The plan proposed formulae to end the civil strife in individual countries, achieving this aim first in Nicaragua (1989), then in El Salvador (1991). In Guatemala, a ceasefire after 36 years of war led to the signing of a peace accord at the end of 1996. With the signing of peace accords, emphasis has shifted to regional, economic and environmental integration.

In October 1993, the presidents of Guatemala, El Salvador, Honduras, Nicaragua and Costa Rica signed a new **Central American Integration Treaty Protocol** to replace that of 1960 and set up new mechanisms for regional integration. The Treaty was the culmination of a series of annual presidential summits held since 1986 which, besides aiming for peace and economic integration, established a Central American Parliament and a Central American Court of Justice. Attempts at further economic and regional integration continue. Plans to create a **Free Trade Area of the Americas** (FTAA) appear to have failed, but the 2003 **Dominican Republic-Central American Free Trade Agreement**

(DR-CAFTA) has now been signed by several nations including the Dominican Republic, Guatemala, El Salvador, Honduras, Nicaragua and Costa Rica.

The DR-CAFTA closely compliments the 2001 **Plan Puebla-Panama** (the PPP, also known as the Mesoamerican Integration and Development Project) an economic corridor stretching from Puebla, west of Mexico City, as far as Panama. Supporters of the plan see it as a means for economic development. Critics see it as a way of draining cheap labour and natural resources with little concern for the environment or long-term progress. Today, the PPP simmers on the back burner, but the desire for Central American nations to strengthen ties is regularly voiced. This is most apparent in the creation of Central America 4 (CA-4), a 2006 border control agreement between Guatemala, El Salvador, Honduras and Nicaragua, that opens up travel between the four nations. Regional meetings occur periodically to promote and encourage trust and cooperation, and while the final destination of such cooperation is far from clear, the Central America of today is far more productive and safer than it was in the 1980s and early 1990s.

El Salvador

History

When Spanish expeditions arrived in El Salvador from Guatemala and Nicaragua, they found it quite densely populated by several indigenous groups, of whom the most populous were the Pipiles. By 1550, the Spaniards had occupied the country, many living in existing indigenous villages and towns. The settlers cultivated cocoa in the volcanic highlands and balsam along the coast, and introduced cattle to roam the grasslands freely. Towards the end of the 16th century, indigo became the big export crop: production was controlled by the Spaniards, and the indigenous population provided the workforce, many suffering illness as a result. A period of regional turmoil accompanied El Salvador's declaration of Independence from the newly autonomous political body of Central America in 1839: indigenous attempts to regain their traditional land rights were put down by force.

Coffee emerged as an important cash crop in the second half of the 19th century, bringing with it improvements in transport facilities and the final abolition of indigenous communal lands.

The land question was a fundamental cause of the peasant uprising of 1932, which was brutally crushed by the dictator **General Maximiliano Hernández Martínez**. Following his overthrow in 1944, the military did not relinquish power: a series of military coups kept them in control, while they protected the interests of the landowning oligarchy.

1980s Civil War

The most recent military coup, in October 1979, led to the formation of a civilian-military junta which promised far-reaching reforms. When these were not carried out, the opposition unified forming a broad coalition, the Frente Democrático Revolucionario, which adopted a military wing, the **Farabundo Martí National Liberation Front (FMLN)** in 1980. Later the same year, the Christian Democrat **Ingeniero José Napoleón Duarte** was named as President of the Junta. At about the same time, political tension reached the proportions of civil war.

Duarte was elected to the post of president in 1984, following a short administration headed by Dr Alvaro Magaña. Duarte's periods of power were characterized by a partly successful attempt at land reform, the nationalization of foreign trade and the banking system, and violence. In addition to deaths in combat, 40,000 civilians were killed between 1979 and 1984, mostly by right-wing death squads. Among the casualties was **Archbishop Oscar Romero**, who was shot while saying mass in March 1980. Nothing came of meetings between Duarte's government and the FMLN, which were aimed at seeking a peace agreement. The war continued in stalemate until 1989, by which time an estimated 70,000 had been killed. The Christian Democrats' inability to end the war, reverse the economic decline or rebuild after the 1986 earthquake, combined with their reputation for corruption, brought about a resurgence of support for the right-wing National Republican Alliance (ARENA). An FMLN offer to participate in presidential elections, dependent on certain conditions, was not accepted and the ARENA candidate, **Alfredo Cristiani**, won the presidency comfortably in March 1989, taking office in June. Peace talks again failed to produce results and in November 1989 the FMLN guerrillas staged their most ambitious offensive ever, which paralysed the capital and caused a violent backlash from government forces. FMLN-government negotiations resumed with UN mediation following the offensive, but the two sides could not reach agreement about the purging of the armed forces, which had become the most wealthy institution in the country following 10 years of US support.

Peace negotiations

Although El Salvador's most left-wing political party, the Unión Democrática Nacionalista, agreed to participate in municipal elections in 1991, the FMLN remained outside the electoral process, and the civil war continued unresolved. Talks were held in Venezuela and Mexico after initial agreement was reached in April on reforms to the electoral and judicial systems, but further progress was stalled over the restructuring of the armed forces and disarming the guerrillas. There were hopes that human rights would improve after the establishment in June 1991 of a UN Security Council human rights observer commission (ONUSAL), which was charged with verifying compliance with the human rights agreement signed by the Government and the FMLN in Geneva in April 1990. Finally, after considerable UN assistance, the FMLN and the Government signed a peace accord in New York in January 1992 and a formal ceasefire began the following month. A detailed schedule throughout 1992 was established to demobilize the FMLN, dismantle five armed forces elite battalions and to initiate land requests by ex-combatants from both sides. The demobilization process was reported as completed in December 1992, formally concluding the civil war. The US agreed at this point to 'forgive' a substantial portion of the US$2 billion international debt of El Salvador. In March 1993, the United Nations Truth Commission published its investigation of human rights abuses during the civil war. Five days later, the legislature approved a general amnesty for all those involved in criminal activities in the war. This included those named in the Truth Commission report. The Cristiani government was slow to implement not only the constitutional reforms proposed by the Truth Commission, but also the process of land reform and the establishment of the National Civilian Police (PNC). By 1995, when Cristiani's successor had taken office, the old national police force was demobilized, but the PNC suffered from a lack of resources for its proper establishment. In fact, the budget for the implementation of the final peace accords was inadequate and El Salvador had to ask the UN for financial assistance.

1994 elections and after

Presidential and congressional elections in 1994 failed to give an outright majority to any presidential candidate and **Calderón Sol** of ARENA won the run-off election. Besides his government's difficulties with the final stages of the peace accord, his first months in office were marked by rises in the cost of living, increases in crime, strikes and protests, and occupations of the Legislature by ex-combatants. Frustration at the slow rate of reform came in the form of criticism from the United Nations and in March 1997 through the ballot box. Only 41% of the electorate bothered to vote. In the National Assembly, Arena won 29 seats, narrowly beating the FMLN which increased its tally to 28 seats. The National Conciliation Party (PCN) won 11, the Christian Democrats (PDC) nine and minority parties seven seats. FMLN managed to run neck-and-neck with Arena until within a year of the March 1999 presidential elections. The party's inability to select a presidential candidate, however, caused it to lose ground rapidly. Arena's candidate, **Fransisco Flores**, won the election but still with a poor turn-out of less than 40% of the electorate. In the face of such a huge rejection of the political system Flores could not claim a clear mandate. Most interpreted the abstention as a lack of faith in any party's ability to solve the twin problems of poverty and crime. Elections in March 2004 won a five-year term for **Tony Saca**, the fourth successive victory for the right-wing Arena party. The former radio and TV presenter promised to crack down on criminal gangs and promote ties with the US.

Into the 21st century

If the devastating earthquakes of early 2001 were not enough for the country to deal with, droughts through the summer months led to a food crisis that required United Nations' intervention. Old rivalries flared briefly as Honduras expelled two Salvadorean diplomats on spying charges, displaying the fragility of the cordial relations with the northern neighbour. El Salvador also hosted the meeting of Mexican and Central America presidents to develop the controversial **Plan Puebla-Panama** regional integration project which would link the Mexican city of Puebla with Panama City along an economic investment corridor. In 2002, promising signs of progress and support for the future led US President Bush to call El Salvador one of the "really bright lights" in the region.

The country's lively landscape continued to shape events with the eruption of Ilamatepec volcano, also known as Santa Ana, in October 2005, quickly followed by the destructive floods and mudslides of Hurricane Stan which killed over 70 people, and forced over 36,000 to seek refuge in emergency shelters. In 2006 El Salvador continued to lead the way for regional integration as the first country to fully implement the Central American Free Trade Agreement with the US. The regional confidence continued and El Salvador and Honduras inaugurated their newly defined border in April 2006, bringing to an end the dispute that led to the outbreak of war between the two nations in 1969. In March 2011, the Inter-American Commission on Human Rights prepared to reopen the court case investigating the massacre of some 1000 civilians in village of El Mozote in December 1981, the bloodiest episode in the country's civil war. In the same month, US President Barack Obama offered US$200m to help El Salvador fight drug traffickers and gang violence. The money is part of the $1.5bn 'Mérida Initiative' announced in 2007 to combat the drugs cartels.

Culture

People

The population of 6.7 million people is far more homogeneous than that of Guatemala. The reason for this is that El Salvador lay comparatively isolated from the main stream of conquest, and had no precious metals to act as magnets for the Spaniards. The small number of Spanish settlers intermarried with those indigenous locals who survived the plagues brought from Europe to form a group of mestizos. There were only about half a million people as late as 1879. With the introduction of coffee, the population grew quickly and the new prosperity fertilized the whole economy, but the internal pressure of population has led to the occupation of all the available land. Several hundred thousand Salvadoreans have emigrated to neighbouring republics because of the shortage of land and the concentration of land ownership, and, more recently, because of the civil war.

Of the total population, some 10% are regarded as ethnic indigenous, although the traditional indigenous culture has almost completely vanished. Other estimates put the percentage of the pure indigenous population as low as 5%. The Lenca and the Pipil, the two surviving indigenous groups, are predominantly peasant farmers. Only 1% are of unmixed white ancestry, the rest are mestizos.

With a population of 322 to the square kilometre, El Salvador is the most densely populated country on the American mainland. Health and sanitation outside the capital and some of the main towns leave much to be desired.

Music and dance

The Mexican music industry seems to exert an overwhelming cultural influence, while the virtual absence of an indigenous population may also be partly responsible, since it is so often they who maintain traditions and connections with the past. Whatever the reason, the visitor who is seeking specifically Salvadorean native music will find little to satisfy him or her. El Salvador is an extension of 'marimba country', but songs and dances are often accompanied by the guitar and seem to lack a rhythm or style that can be pinpointed as specifically local. An exception is the music played on the *pito de caña* and *tambor* which accompanies the traditional dances called *Danza de los Historiantes*, *La Historia* or *Los Moros y Cristianos*. Over 30 types of dance have been identified, mostly in the west and centre of the country, although there are a few in the east. The main theme is the conflict between christianized and 'heretic' *indígenas* and the dances are performed as a ritual on the local saint's day.

Education and religion

State education is free and nominally obligatory. There are 43 universities, three national and the others private or church-affiliated. There is also a National School of Agriculture. The most famous are the government-financed Universidad Nacional and the Jesuit-run Universidad Centroamericana. Roman Catholicism is the prevailing religion.

Land and environment

El Salvador is the smallest, most densely populated and most integrated of the Central American republics. Its intermont basins are a good deal lower than those of Guatemala, rising to little more than 600 m at the capital, San Salvador. Across this upland and surmounting it run two more or less parallel rows of volcanoes, 14% of which are over 900 m high. The highest are Santa Ana (2365 m), San Vicente (2182 m), San Miguel (2130 m), and San Salvador (1893 m). One important result of this volcanic activity is that the highlands are covered with a deep layer of ash and lava which forms a porous soil ideal for coffee planting.

The total area of El Salvador is 21,000 sq km. Guatemala is to the west, Honduras to the north and east, and the Pacific coastline to the south is approximately 321 km long. Lowlands lie to the north and south of the high backbone. In the south, on the Pacific coast, the lowlands of Guatemala are confined to just east of Acajutla; beyond are lava promontories before another 30-km belt of lowlands where the 325-km long Río Lempa flows into the sea. The northern lowlands are in the wide depression along the course of the Río Lempa, buttressed to the south by the highlands of El Salvador and to the north by the basalt cliffs edging the highlands of Honduras. The highest point in El Salvador, Cerro El Pital (2730 m) is part of the mountain range bordering on Honduras. After 160 km the Lempa cuts through the southern uplands to reach the Pacific; the depression is prolonged southeast till it reaches the Gulf of Fonseca.

El Salvador is located on the southwest coast of the Central American Isthmus on the Pacific Ocean. As the only country in the region lacking access to the Caribbean Sea, it does not posses the flora associated with that particular coastal zone. El Salvador nevertheless has a wide variety of colourful, tropical vegetation; for example over 200 species of orchid grow all over the country. As a result of excessive forest cutting, and hence the destruction of their habitats, many of the animals (such as jaguars and crested eagles) once found in the highlands of the country, have diminished at an alarming rate. In response to this problem several nature reserves have been set up in areas where flora and fauna can be found in their most unspoilt state. Among these nature reserves are the Cerro Verde, Deininger Park, El Imposible Woods, El Jocatal Lagoon and the Montecristo Cloud Forest.

Books and films

Books
Argueta, Manlio *One day of Life* (1980) and *Cuzcatlán* (1986). A look at peasant rebellion during El Salvador's 20th-century history.
Raudales, Walter *Amor de Jade*. To be published in English too, is a novel based on the life of El Salvador's Mata Hari (now ex-comandante Joaquín Villalobos' wife).

Films
Romero (1989). Covers the story surrounding the archbishop's assassination. Starring Raúl Julia.
Salvador (1986). Oliver's Stone film takes the journalist's view of events in the country's civil war circa 1980.

Contents

Footnotes

Basic Spanish for travellers

Learning Spanish is a useful part of the preparation for a trip to Latin America and no volumes of dictionaries, phrase books or word lists will provide the same enjoyment as being able to communicate directly with the people of the country you are visiting. It is a good idea to make an effort to grasp the basics before you go. As you travel you will pick up more of the language and the more you know, the more you will benefit from your stay.

General pronunciation

Whether you have been taught the 'Castilian' pronunciation (*z* and *c* followed by *i* or *e* are pronounced as the *th* in think) or the 'American' pronunciation (they are pronounced as *s*), you will encounter little difficulty in understanding either. Regional accents and usages vary, but the basic language is essentially the same everywhere.

Vowels

a	as in English *cat*
e	as in English *best*
i	as the *ee* in English *feet*
o	as in English *shop*
u	as the *oo* in English *food*
ai	as the *i* in English *ride*
ei	as *ey* in English *they*
oi	as *oy* in English *toy*

Consonants

Most consonants can be pronounced more or less as they are in English. The exceptions are:

g	before *e* or *i* is the same as *j*
h	is always silent (except in *ch* as in *chair*)
j	as the *ch* in Scottish *loch*
ll	as the *y* in *yellow*
ñ	as the *ni* in English *onion*
rr	trilled much more than in English
x	depending on its location, pronounced *x, s, sh* or *j*

Spanish words and phrases

Greetings, courtesies

hello	*hola*	please	*por favor*
good morning	*buenos días*	thank you (very much)	*(muchas) gracias*
good afternoon/		I don't speak Spanish	*no hablo español*
evening/night	*buenas tardes/noches*	do you speak English?	*¿habla inglés?*
		I don't understand	*no comprendo*
goodbye	*adiós/chao*	please speak slowly	*hable despacio por favor*
pleased to meet you	*mucho gusto*		
see you later	*hasta luego*	I am very sorry	*lo siento mucho*
how are you?	*¿cómo está?*	what do you want?	*¿qué quiere?*
	¿cómo estás?		*¿qué quieres?*
I'm fine, thanks	*estoy muy bien, gracias*	I want	*quiero*
I'm called...	*me llamo...*	I don't want it	*no lo quiero*
what is your name?	*¿cómo se llama?*	leave me alone	*déjeme en paz/*
	¿cómo te llamas?		*no me moleste*
yes/no	*sí/no*	good/bad	*bueno/malo*

Questions and requests

Have you got a room for two people?
¿Tiene una habitación para dos personas?
How do I get to_? *¿Cómo llego a_?*
How much does it cost?
¿Cuánto cuesta? ¿cuánto es?
I'd like to make a long-distance phone call
Quisiera hacer una llamada de larga distancia
Is service included? *¿Está incluido el servicio?*
Is tax included? *¿Están incluidos los impuestos?*

When does the bus leave (arrive)?
¿A qué hora sale (llega) el autobús?
When? *¿cuándo?*
Where is_? *¿dónde está_?*
Where can I buy tickets?
¿Dónde puedo comprar boletos?
Where is the nearest petrol station?
¿Dónde está la gasolinera más cercana?
Why? *¿por qué?*

Basics

bank	*el banco*	market	*el mercado*
bathroom/toilet	*el baño*	note/coin	*el billete/la moneda*
bill	*la factura/la cuenta*	police (policeman)	*la policía (el policía)*
cash	*el efectivo*	post office	*el correo*
cheap	*barato/a*	public telephone	*el teléfono público*
credit card	*la tarjeta de crédito*	supermarket	*el supermercado*
exchange house	*la casa de cambio*	ticket office	*la taquilla*
exchange rate	*el tipo de cambio*	traveller's cheques	*los cheques de*
expensive	*caro/a*		*viajero/los travelers*

Getting around

aeroplane	*el avión*	insured person	*el/la asegurado/a*
airport	*el aeropuerto*	to insure yourself against	*asegurarse contra*
arrival/departure	*la llegada/salida*	luggage	*el equipaje*
avenue	*la avenida*	motorway, freeway	*el autopista/la*
block	*la cuadra*		*carretera*
border	*la frontera*	north, south, west, east	*norte, sur,*
bus station	*la terminal de*		*oeste (occidente),*
	autobuses/camiones		*este (oriente)*
bus	*el bus/el autobús/*	oil	*el aceite*
	el camión	to park	*estacionarse*
collective/		passport	*el pasaporte*
fixed-route taxi	*el colectivo*	petrol/gasoline	*la gasolina*
corner	*la esquina*	puncture	*el pinchazo/*
customs	*la aduana*		*la ponchadura*
first/second class	*primera/segunda clase*	street	*la calle*
left/right	*izquierda/derecha*	that way	*por allí/por allá*
ticket	*el boleto*	this way	*por aquí/por acá*
empty/full	*vacío/lleno*	tourist card/visa	*la tarjeta de turista*
highway, main road	*la carretera*	tyre	*la llanta*
immigration	*la inmigración*	unleaded	*sin plomo*
insurance	*el seguro*	to walk	*caminar/andar*

Accommodation

air conditioning	*el aire acondicionado*	power cut	*el apagón/corte*
all-inclusive	*todo incluido*	restaurant	*el restaurante*
bathroom, private	*el baño privado*	room/bedroom	*el cuarto/l*
bed, double/single	*la cama matrimonial/*		*a habitación*
	sencilla	sheets	*las sábanas*
blankets	*las cobijas/mantas*	shower	*la ducha/regadera*
to clean	*limpiar*	soap	*el jabón*
dining room	*el comedor*	toilet	*el sanitario/excusado*
guesthouse	*la casa de huéspedes*	toilet paper	*el papel higiénico*
hotel	*el hotel*	towels, clean/dirty	*las toallas limpias/*
noisy	*ruidoso*		*sucias*
pillows	*las almohadas*	water, hot/cold	*el agua caliente/fría*

Health

aspirin	*la aspirina*	diarrhoea	*la diarrea*
blood	*la sangre*	doctor	*el médico*
chemist	*la farmacia*	fever/sweat	*la fiebre/el sudor*
condoms	*los preservativos,*	pain	*el dolor*
	los condones	head	*la cabeza*
contact lenses	*los lentes de contacto*	period/	*la regla/*
contraceptives	*los anticonceptivos*	sanitary towels	*las toallas femeninas*
contraceptive pill	*la píldora anti-*	stomach	*el estómago*
	conceptiva	altitude sickness	*el soroche*

Family

family	*la familia*	boyfriend/girlfriend	*el novio/la novia*
brother/sister	*el hermano/la hermana*	friend	*el amigo/la amiga*
daughter/son	*la hija/el hijo*	married	*casado/a*
father/mother	*el padre/la madre*	single/unmarried	*soltero/a*
husband/wife	*el esposo (marido)/*		
	la esposa		

Months, days and time

January	*enero*	November	*noviembre*
February	*febrero*	December	*diciembre*
March	*marzo*		
April	*abril*	Monday	*lunes*
May	*mayo*	Tuesday	*martes*
June	*junio*	Wednesday	*miércoles*
July	*julio*	Thursday	*jueves*
August	*agosto*	Friday	*viernes*
September	*septiembre*	Saturday	*sábado*
October	*octubre*	Sunday	*domingo*

at one o'clock	*a la una*	it's six twenty	*son las seis y veinte*
at half past two	*a las dos y media*	it's five to nine	*son las nueve menos*
at a quarter to three	*a cuarto para las tres/*		*cinco*
	a las tres menos quince	in ten minutes	*en diez minutos*
it's one o'clock	*es la una*	five hours	*cinco horas*
it's seven o'clock	*son las siete*	does it take long?	*¿tarda mucho?*

Numbers

one	*uno/una*	sixteen	*dieciséis*
two	*dos*	seventeen	*diecisiete*
three	*tres*	eighteen	*dieciocho*
four	*cuatro*	nineteen	*diecinueve*
five	*cinco*	twenty	*veinte*
six	*seis*	twenty-one	*veintiuno*
seven	*siete*	thirty	*treinta*
eight	*ocho*	forty	*cuarenta*
nine	*nueve*	fifty	*cincuenta*
ten	*diez*	sixty	*sesenta*
eleven	*once*	seventy	*setenta*
twelve	*doce*	eighty	*ochenta*
thirteen	*trece*	ninety	*noventa*
fourteen	*catorce*	hundred	*cien/ciento*
fifteen	*quince*	thousand	*mil*

Food

avocado	*el aguacate*	fish	*el pescado*
baked	*al horno*	fork	*el tenedor*
bakery	*la panadería*	fried	*frito*
banana	*el plátano*	garlic	*el ajo*
beans	*los frijoles/*	goat	*el chivo*
	las habichuelas	grapefruit	*la toronja/el pomelo*
beef	*la carne de res*	grill	*la parrilla*
beef steak or pork fillet	*el bistec*	grilled/griddled	*a la plancha*
boiled rice	*el arroz blanco*	guava	*la guayaba*
bread	*el pan*	ham	*el jamón*
breakfast	*el desayuno*	hamburger	*la hamburguesa*
butter	*la mantequilla*	hot, spicy	*picante*
cake	*el pastel*	ice cream	*el helado*
chewing gum	*el chicle*	jam	*la mermelada*
chicken	*el pollo*	knife	*el cuchillo*
chilli or green pepper	*el ají/pimiento*	lime	*el limón*
clear soup, stock	*el caldo*	lobster	*la langosta*
cooked	*cocido*	lunch	*el almuerzo/la comida*
dining room	*el comedor*	meal	*la comida*
egg	*el huevo*	meat	*la carne*

minced meat	*el picadillo*	sausage	*la longaniza/el chorizo*
onion	*la cebolla*	scrambled eggs	*los huevos revueltos*
orange	*la naranja*	seafood	*los mariscos*
pepper	*el pimiento*	soup	*la sopa*
pasty, turnover	*la empanada/*	spoon	*la cuchara*
	el pastelito	squash	*la calabaza*
pork	*el cerdo*	squid	*los calamares*
potato	*la papa*	supper	*la cena*
prawns	*los camarones*	sweet	*dulce*
raw	*crudo*	to eat	*comer*
restaurant	*el restaurante*	toasted	*tostado*
salad	*la ensalada*	turkey	*el pavo*
salt	*la sal*	vegetables	*los legumbres/vegetales*
sandwich	*el bocadillo*	without meat	*sin carne*
sauce	*la salsa*	yam	*el camote*

Drink

beer	*la cerveza*	ice/without ice	*el hielo/sin hielo*
boiled	*hervido/a*	juice	*el jugo*
bottled	*en botella*	lemonade	*la limonada*
camomile tea	*la manzanilla*	milk	*la leche*
canned	*en lata*	mint	*la menta*
coffee	*el café*	rum	*el ron*
coffee, white	*el café con leche*	soft drink	*el refresco*
cold	*frío*	sugar	*el azúcar*
cup	*la taza*	tea	*el té*
drink	*la bebida*	to drink	*beber/tomar*
drunk	*borracho/a*	water	*el agua*
firewater	*el aguardiente*	water, carbonated	*el agua mineral con gas*
fruit milkshake	*el batido/licuado*	water, still mineral	*el agua mineral sin gas*
glass	*el vaso*	wine, red	*el vino tinto*
hot	*caliente*	wine, white	*el vino blanco*

Key verbs

to go	**ir**
I go	voy
you go (familiar)	vas
he, she, it goes, you (formal) go	va
we go	vamos
they, you (plural) go	van

to have (possess)	**tener**
I have	tengo
you (familiar) have	tienes
he, she, it, you (formal) have	tiene
we have	tenemos
they, you (plural) have	tienen

there is/are	hay
there isn't/aren't	no hay

to be	**ser**	estar
I am	soy	estoy
you are	eres	estás
he, she, it is, you (formal) are	es	está
we are	somos	estamos
they, you (plural) are	son	están

This section has been assembled on the basis of glossaries compiled by André de Mendonça and David Gilmour of South American Experience, London, and the Latin American Travel Advisor, No 9, March 1996

Index

Titles available in the Footprint *Focus* range

Latin America	UK RRP	US RRP
Bahia & Salvador	£7.99	$11.95
Buenos Aires & Pampas	£7.99	$11.95
Costa Rica	£8.99	$12.95
Cuzco, La Paz & Lake Titicaca	£8.99	$12.95
El Salvador	£5.99	$8.95
Guadalajara & Pacific Coast	£6.99	$9.95
Guatemala	£8.99	$12.95
Guyana, Guyane & Suriname	£5.99	$8.95
Havana	£6.99	$9.95
Honduras	£7.99	$11.95
Nicaragua	£7.99	$11.95
Paraguay	£5.99	$8.95
Quito & Galápagos Islands	£7.99	$11.95
Recife & Northeast Brazil	£7.99	$11.95
Rio de Janeiro	£8.99	$12.95
São Paulo	£5.99	$8.95
Uruguay	£6.99	$9.95
Venezuela	£8.99	$12.95
Yucatán Peninsula	£6.99	$9.95

Asia	UK RRP	US RRP
Angkor Wat	£5.99	$8.95
Bali & Lombok	£8.99	$12.95
Chennai & Tamil Nadu	£8.99	$12.95
Chiang Mai & Northern Thailand	£7.99	$11.95
Goa	£6.99	$9.95
Hanoi & Northern Vietnam	£8.99	$12.95
Ho Chi Minh City & Mekong Delta	£7.99	$11.95
Java	£7.99	$11.95
Kerala	£7.99	$11.95
Kolkata & West Bengal	£5.99	$8.95
Mumbai & Gujarat	£8.99	$12.95

Africa & Middle East	UK RRP	US RRP
Beirut	£6.99	$9.95
Damascus	£5.99	$8.95
Durban & KwaZulu Natal	£8.99	$12.95
Fès & Northern Morocco	£8.99	$12.95
Jerusalem	£8.99	$12.95
Johannesburg & Kruger National Park	£7.99	$11.95
Kenya's beaches	£8.99	$12.95
Kilimanjaro & Northern Tanzania	£8.99	$12.95
Zanzibar & Pemba	£7.99	$11.95

Europe	UK RRP	US RRP
Bilbao & Basque Region	£6.99	$9.95
Granada & Sierra Nevada	£6.99	$9.95
Málaga	£5.99	$8.95
Orkney & Shetland Islands	£5.99	$8.95
Skye & Outer Hebrides	£6.99	$9.95

North America	UK RRP	US RRP
Vancouver & Rockies	£8.99	$12.95

Australasia	UK RRP	US RRP
Brisbane & Queensland	£8.99	$12.95
Perth	£7.99	$11.95

For the latest books, e-books and smart phone app releases, and a wealth of travel information, visit us at:
www.footprinttravelguides.com.

footprinttravelguides.com

Join us on facebook for the latest travel news, product releases, offers and amazing competitions: www.facebook.com/footprintbooks.com.